To John

Holly Renul

At Home:
The Incredible Story of
The Welcome Mission

A Memoir of Ministry

By Holly Rench

Theo Media

2019

In writing this memoir, I have recreated events, locales and conversations from my memories of them. I have changed the names of individuals and places, and in some places changed identifying characteristics and details such as physical properties, occupations and places of residence.

Cover Art by Laurie Duncan

First Edition

This book is dedicated to Marcus, Alex and Theo. The three of you made The Welcome Mission possible. You not only allowed me to bring absolute strangers into our home to live, but you embraced them (and others) as members of our family.

You're all truly remarkable.

Contents

Postscript
I'm Still Dreaming - The Future of TWM

Appendix
Acknowledgements
Holly's Reading Table
Ma's Recipes from TWM
TWM Playlist
About the Author

You can give without loving,
but you cannot love without giving.

- Amy Carmichael

Introduction

If I could wave a magic wand, and make something become true, it would be for anything I say in this book to inspire people to love and good works.

How do you begin to help people see that these dear souls are precious in His sight and they desperately need to be accepted and loved, and not ever shunned for being different or for not "looking the part" of a Christian?

I hate it when I hear about Christian people berating others because of their tattoos, or their dyed hair, or their lifestyle. Please think about how the hearer of that would respond! It drives them away from God. Every. Last. Time.

A single self-righteous mother or father can bring down the whole family through their berating and shaming. Their words can make someone (especially a child) believe that there is no chance in hell that God would love them, so they might as well go for all they can get here on earth. This is so tragic. The pedestal they're on is way more evil than anything their target could be doing. And it's so destructive.

How do I know this? I am a recovering self-righteous hypocrite too. I have mistreated my fair share of people because I thought I was better than them. How does this sound, "I am better than you because you're gay. I slept with my heterosexual partner before marriage, but that's somehow better."

At our table today, we had a lonely schizophrenic male in his 20's here, a severely battered young woman, three victims of child sexual abuse (one with pink hair and one with blue), one girl that recently tried to commit suicide, and a heroin addict, enjoying one another's company, over a delicious meal.

These are the Christian castaways. They're the injured one by the road in the parable of the Good Samaritan.

Will you choose to see beyond the blue hair, the piercings and all the shocking language, to see these lovely, special people just waiting even screaming to be loved?

They want a hug. They want comfort and encouragement. They need close connection and intimate friendship. That is how they will see God.

If you show them love and kindness, they will see Jesus because he is loving and kind to the wounded and oppressed.

Or will you wound them further?

Will you condemn them to eternal damnation because they have black fingernail polish?

Will we, as a church, continue to disregard these people that Jesus himself loves?

Love them like Jesus does. There's mercy for them just like there's mercy for you, and all of us.

This book is intended to help you do just that. It's to help you see all humans as valuable. For too long, the church has looked down on the poor, the addict, the prostitute, and any myriad of other nouns that describe someone that's living a life that's beneath those of the "good" congregants. I lived in that mindset for so much of my life too.

Now, when I see someone on the street corner, or tweaking, or homeless, I think about what that dear person must be going through and how I would like to help. I think about how there aren't enough soldiers of God's love and mercy.

We need an army! The harvest is huge and overwhelming. Most days, the overwhelming-ness of it overtakes me. Where is His army? Right now, I see an uprising though, in the camp. People with big hearts, who know about God's mercy on their own lives, are willing to abandon their desires and their love of money to be all in for Jesus and His kingdom.

I see messy people pushing back the gates of hell through self sacrifice and love. We won't do it through politics, I hate to tell some folks. "With deeds of love and mercy" as the great hymn, Lead On Oh King Eternal says. The problem is, deeds of love and mercy are hard to do. It requires so much more of you.

As I write this tonight, I'm a nervous wreck. I have a new girl coming in tomorrow. She's a heroin addict that's been in rehab. To be honest, I don't want to do it.

This is hard stuff and I can't keep thinking about what a mess I am and who am I to be entrusted with this messed up soul? Then, my thinking turns to the thoughts of the possibility that God can use us to really make a change in her life.

Wow. That's a game changer. This girl is my daughter's age. She already reminds me of her. I feel like I'm helping Kat, which I cannot do. You'll hear more about her in a little while.

This little book is filled with stories of so many of my girls, told from my perspective. It tells the highs and the lows with honesty. It speaks from my heart and it's raw. I've tried to be as transparent and honest as much as possible.

I hope you're inspired to good works and entertained as I tell of this crazy, love-filled, grace-infused, messy, shit-show called life here at The Welcome Mission (TWM). Y'all relax...it's just a four letter word. It's alright.

Prologue
(The Girls, in Their Own Words)

Merry

I remember the day I stopped being happy. I remember feeling waves of sadness, and I hated myself. This was the beginning of a depression I still struggle with daily.

I began trying to find ways to numb myself at a young age. I spiraled out of control, barely graduated high school and flunked out of college.

My drug use and unhealthy behaviors eventually caught up to me, and I ended up in jail facing serious charges. I called my mom from the jail as I did everyday. She told me I'd be going to rehab in California. Best news of my life.

I went and made beautiful friends in a beautiful place and made a great transition in my life. My parents knew I couldn't go back to my hometown and live a sober life so quickly out of rehab.

My grandfather had a connection with some people in North Carolina who ran a sort of "safe place" if you will, out of their own home. It was The Welcome Mission.

So, here I am, close to four months later. Happier than I've ever been, and living a life close to these amazing people and even closer to Jesus. I haven't felt such stability in my life in a very long time.

And it's all thanks to my family here: Ma, Pa, Alex and Theo Rench. And of course my beautiful sisters Hope, Vanessa and K.

I know the future holds great things for me, even though it looked so bleak just a short while ago. They encourage me every day to love myself like they love me.

I'm forever grateful for the love, grace and compassion The Welcome Mission has given me.

Vanessa

My time at The Welcome Mission is coming to an end. With that comes reflection. The past four years are my most defining years. I'll break it down into four themes:

Before my senior year of high school I surrendered to Christ. It was the first time I felt I had a purpose and at the time you could say I had one hell of a "Christian resume." It didn't last.

One bad night led to years of darkness. Making choice after choice leading deeper into the darkness.. I asked Him to free me but I refused to accept that freedom. He didn't make it easy to make those choices but I was stubborn. Then I was pregnant. Stubborn and pregnant. Depraved.

Now let's think about it: here I am, this young girl living my life in constant sin. Different guys in and out of my life, surrounded by people just as depraved as I was, and God gives me a child? Grace!

Grace so beautiful, grace so freeing, grace so endless I finally realized He had already beat my depravity. Grace so powerful it knocked me to my knees in complete surrender. Laying all of my darkness at His feet. Trusting in His redemptive power and desiring to serve Him. Repentance.

Here I find myself desiring to be near to my Lord, yet I am still living in circumstances and associating myself with people seeking to serve themselves.

Insert The Welcome Mission. Marcus (Pa) and Holly (Ma) agreed to welcome me and soon-to-be K into their home. The first day I was able to experience the depths of their love: February 14th. Can't deny the beauty of that. Living with these phenomenal people has required some deep internal work to be done. Not my favorite thing. Yet, the accountability that I have received I have seen Jesus use. Making me more like Him. Sanctification.

There are a few things I can say about the past few years.

Jesus is Who He says He is.

His Grace is abundant.

There's hope.

Lastly, without Ma and Pa I don't know that my resolve to pursue Christ would have stuck. Without their guidance, encouragement, love, and enormous amounts of grace I could honestly say I would have eventually fallen back into the cycle.

They are my example. They are my living and breathing version of the Bible. The thought that my time here is almost up is terrifying. I'm not quite sure I am ready but I am thankfully less than a mile away. I still need their accountability.

The truth is I am here because of their desire to follow Christ into the trenches. To walk life with others and to fellowship with the least of these. I will be forever grateful. Thank you.

Garden of Eden

To many, Valentine's Day is known as the holiday we celebrate with our romantic partners, but for me it's Day One of my journey to truly understanding unconditional love. It's the day I moved into The Welcome Mission; my first day at home. Our concept of home, or what makes a home, is greatly impacted by our personal experiences and understanding.

For some, home is defined but who you live with, yet, to others home is defined by what you feel when you walk through the door. If we look at the first two chapters of Genesis, we may find that God destined home for something greater than we have ever been able to fathom. Home is where we dwell with Him; surrounded by His presence!

The Garden of Eden was the first home created by God. Adam and Eve had complete access to an unlimited supply of food. They were able to enjoy each others company endlessly. Free of shame. Free of fear. Not a single worry. They walked in the presence of the Trinity, experiencing every aspect of who He is all at once.

After they ate the apple, everything changed. We toil for our food. We fight for time from our loved ones. There's always something about ourselves to be ashamed of, always something to be worried about, and peace seems unattainable at times.

We are desperately fighting to have one place to go to, one place where it all washes away, one place where we feel free.

Home. We just want to be home. So we fight desperately to create our space, but if we are honest something is always missing. He is missing.

When God gave Adam and Eve the garden and all its benefits, they did what we do daily. They missed the point. The Garden of Eden wasn't created solely for the purpose of their comfort, but instead, as a place to be among Him. A place for us to dwell in His presence.

In your hands you have something I am so thankful for, our stories. As a former Welcome Mission girl, I am thrilled for anyone who is interested to learn about the transformation of Jesus in my life. To see how that transformation took place because two people decided we all need Jesus as much as the others and did something about it. The concept of opening their house is where people call them saints. I call them saints because they did not just open their house, they opened themselves. They could have stopped with opening the door and patted themselves on the back, but instead they poured everything they had into us. They showed us Jesus. They showed us what a house with Him at the center looks like: home.

There is no doubt in my mind as you read these pages, that you will find your emotions are splattered all over the wall. At times you may be laughing, sometimes sad, other times joyous, and even at moments, angry. All of those feelings could be felt for a myriad of reasons. Whether that's because you are feeling what was truly felt in the moment, or because you deeply disagree with the methods, I urge you to read on.

I urge you to remember that unconditional love is messy for all involved. I urge you to pray for the Rench's and their girls. I urge you to remember how magnificently He can use all the things that seem wrong for beauty.

Most of all, I urge you to hear me when I say not every part of living at The Welcome Mission felt beautiful, but for every moment on my own, I am more than thankful for all of the hard things, all the lessons, and all the unconditional love.

Last but not least, I pray that as you read your eyes are open to how God is working at The Welcome Mission, the necessity of what they are doing, and you are reminded of just how amazing grace truly is.

Stories and Journeys

1
Beauty Found Here

If you want to go fast, go alone.
If you want to go far, go together.
- African Proverb

My hope in writing this book is to inspire others to directly minister to their neighbors that are in need. I don't want to scare anyone off with the true picture of life at TWM, but I do want to be transparent about it. It's hard.

Let me tell you about the beauty. I want to paint a picture for you of the lovely things about these girls and our relationships with them.

One night Marcus and I were sitting up in the bed watching tv. In walks one of the girls, followed by two more. They had questions to ask "Ma" and so they ended up sitting all around. One sat on the stationary bike that never got used, and two sat on the end of the bed.

The scene was absolutely hilarious to me. Here were our "adopted" full grown adult children, sitting around "Ma" and "Pa," having casual conversation like a "normal" family.

I snapped a picture because it was so poignant and it made my heart smile. That was exactly what I wanted to achieve! A sense of family. And there it was.

I can remember other evenings, where I was in my room and overheard the chatter and the laughing coming from the kitchen, the girls making pizza or cookies, talking about their day, playing loud music and always dancing.

Those moments made me tear up because those relationships are meaningful and lifelong. They shared life together, even if for a short time. Those bonds are strong, even after moving out and away.

One particular source of beauty in the house comes from Theo. He's our 18 year old son who has Down Syndrome and Autism. He's non-verbal, but his eyes and smile can light up the room. He has been the greatest source of love in this house. It couldn't be the way it is, without him.

The girls quickly get comfortable with a special kid like Theo once they've been around him some. He dances with them and they shower him with hugs and kisses.

On any given day, you'd see one girl holding his hand or another one grabbing him for a hug. Imagine the depth of love they might have even felt for the first time from someone that only Theo can give.

He has taught me more about God than any other human. His perfect image of God in his face and the way he loves unconditionally, have changed me for the good, and I know he's had a huge impact on their lives. You'll learn more about Theo later.

Something we try to teach here and to learn better for ourselves is to die to yourself. Make it your mission to think of and do for others, even if it costs you. So, to see these girls putting one another before themselves at times, is a beautiful thing to see. It doesn't happen all the time, but it begins to happen more and more as they grow.

Family meals together have been beautiful and we have cookouts all summer long and one summer, we were all trying to eat Keto! Meat for dinner every night, folks! Cooked on the grill, then eaten right there at the outside table, often with our fingers.

But there's beauty in feasting too, which was on Sundays and holidays. Some girls came here and would reject homemade lasagna for frozen fish sticks. Fish sticks. Or they would prefer Ramen over my huge salad!

Over time, they begin to enjoy feasting more and more. Their taste buds got retrained and they enjoyed real, delicious food more and more. One Thanksgiving, we had Crawfish Etoufee and gumbo!

Movie nights! We often sit in the living room for movie night, which could also be termed "This Is Us" night. Pa would join us all, often complaining about the sensitivity of the show, and then end up crying with the rest of us. He's actually a softy. You just have to see it under all that grumpiness.

Birthdays are big here, also. I've always done birthday up big for my kids growing up and once I realized that a lot of our girls have never even had a birthday party, I decided it was game on.

It's also a lovely thing to see one another forgive. When we lash out at someone, or get impatient and irritated with one another, I've seen many times where there are tears, apologies and hugs. Forgiveness. Not pretending to be perfect and sliding sin under the rug, but bringing it to the light and quickly forgiving one another.

I had one girl once smoke pot on my back porch, then she felt so guilty that she immediately woke me up, high as a kite, to confess and apologize. That's the kind of thing I can live with.

2
How It All Started

A really strong woman accepts the war
she went through and is ennobled by her scars.
- Carly Simon

In August of 1983, we were married. I was 18. Marcus
turned 26 the day after we wed. I was very immature,
and I mean very. The man I married was, and is, patient
and kind to me. I frankly don't know how he managed
life with me.

I was under the illusion as a Christian, that if you do everything "right", then all would be well. Just obey God.
This teaching, along with lots of pride on my part set me
up for years of torment, shock and sadness.

I thought we would dance our way through life, having
perfect kids and being successful in whatever we did.
But it was more like Andrew Peterson's song, "Let's Go
Dancing In The Minefields." There were definitely minefields and even a few explosions!

As a pastor's family, you don't show weakness. You
can't show sin in your life. It's exhausting trying to keep
up appearances. I put so much pressure on my kids to
perform and look the part that I was playing, because of
how people would view me. I had to look as good as the
pedestal I had erected for myself.

I was to be the example of godliness! In fact, I wasn't at all. But I told myself I was.

Well, my kids didn't always adhere to the standard. My first born definitely didn't. Once she entered the teenage years, her acting out began to be something I could no longer hide from the world...or the church.

She was very difficult to control, and keeping her behavior hidden became impossible. I began wondering what we were going to do for a job if Marcus can't be a pastor because our family wasn't perfect. My façade was truly crumbling.

With that came despair for me. My whole life had been based on lies I'd told myself. Oh, how little I knew and understood back then. I had no idea that being open and vulnerable about our weaknesses and struggles means more to people than perceived perfection.

All that does is make you unapproachable and judgmental. I was definitely judgmental. Why couldn't people obey God like I did? But now my daughter is going to ruin everything. That's how I saw it. How tragic.

I often wonder if we could have changed the course of her life had we seen things differently. What if we had just loved her and not freaked out over any sin in her life? What if we had told her that Jesus loves her no matter what? What if we'd told her that we loved her no matter what?

14

Instead, I got angry because her sin was personal to me, when it was really directed toward God.

For some unknown reason, along the way, throughout the years, people began bringing their teenage daughters to us for help. Yikes! My kids were still quite young. I'm not entirely sure why they brought them, except that we were willing to help.

I had absolutely no idea what in the world to do to help these girls. I had struggled some as a 16-year-old, so maybe these parents thought my experience would be helpful. The very first girl that came to us was while Marcus was in seminary, in 1992. She only stayed a few days. The second girl that came to us was in 1993.

She stayed with us for a few weeks and during that time, I had the privilege of leading her to Christ. I bumbled my way through it and felt quite proud at my accomplishment.

I remember telling my mom over the phone that evening, "Mom! I did it!" That hurts my heart now to remember and write down. But God is so good! He even works through an ass like me! She is married today, has children and is walking faithfully with God.

These patterns kept up, on and off for a while. Then when my own kids got older, their friends that were having problems at home, ended up sometimes coming to me for help of various kinds.

15

In 2010, it got ramped up for various reasons. We had many of our daughter's friends around and everyone seemed to have needs. I did what I could, all the while still trying to navigate my own kids, and often failing at all of it.

Through all of this, something in me was changing. I began to see people differently. My eyes began to be open to the suffering of others in a way that I'd never known before. I often wonder if this was when I was actually saved from my sin instead of knowing him my whole life as I had believed for so long.

I guess the "when" is irrelevant. But the relevant part is that I began having compassion for wounded and op-pressed people, the poor, the broken people.

I used to look at the poor and the broken-down people and wonder why they don't just go to school, *finish* high school, get a decent education and do something with their lives. Here's an interesting, largely unknown fact: I didn't formally finish high school. The hypocrisy behind my thoughts about others is not lost on me.

I worked at the local pregnancy resource center here in Fuquay-Varina and I really saw people for what seemed like the first time. I really saw them!

I heard their stories and saw their pain and realized that I had been missing this aspect of people my whole life!

Something began to stir in me that I'd never felt before. I began to have a burning desire to make a difference in lives. So, I began asking these girls over for Bible studies and for meals. They came! They brought boyfriends too!

I cooked and cooked, and cooked some more. They ate many meals here. They were made to feel as if they could come in, open the refrigerator and help themselves to food anytime they were hungry, just like at home, as long as they washed their hands! That's a "Ma" pet peeve!

I soon began moving them in.

3
Our Town

Alone, we can do so little; together, we can do so much.
- Helen Keller

We live in a small town, about 18 miles south of Raleigh called Fuquay-Varina. In 1963, Fuquay Springs and Varina came together to form one town. When we moved here in 2003, I had no idea how great this little town would be to us.

The folks of Fuquay-Varina have really been good to TWM. I've had the delight to speak at a few of the churches about what we do. Fellowship Bible Church had a Thanksgiving women's lunch and had me speak. One of my girls gave her testimony.

I've also gotten to speak at Redeemer Community Church, and Grace Presbyterian Church. Fuquay Varina United Methodist also let me come and speak to their missions committee.

They've all supported us in different ways. Connect Church has been especially amazing in their care for us. They've sponsored a concert to benefit TWM and they made the video for us that's on our website. Their pastors pray for us and encourage us whenever they can.

I'm forever grateful. Two of their members serve on our TWM board as well.

18

Piney Ridge Baptist Church grows vegetables in the summer and delivers to us loads of them each Saturday during the summer, from their "Garden Of Eaten."

Macedonia Baptist Church comes with their youth group each spring and freshens up our yard with hard work, new plants and pine straw. Nearby, Hope Community Church has raised money for us and also did landscaping for us.

One day last year, we got home from church to about 30 grocery bags full of groceries and supplies of all sorts!

Also, churches outside of Fuquay have done important work for TWM. For example, Stoney Hill Free Will Baptist Church is in process of painting the whole outside of the house! So incredible! They paid for the materials too.

I'm especially encouraged when I see churches be the hands and feet of Jesus in their community.

TWM is our home that we raised our kids in. We're located in the older part of town. Our house is about 60 years old. Lots of houses in this area are in the colonial style.

I preferred the older neighborhoods because the houses are all so different and charming. The trees around us are older and mature. We're about six blocks from downtown. Huge mature camellias and azaleas are everywhere in our neighborhood. It's shaded with a lot of greenery from the large oak and pine trees.

Many girls that have lived here, have been able to walk from TWM to their jobs when necessary.

Several local businesses have supported us and hired some of our girls. Stick Boy Bread Company's owners have sponsored a benefit for us and helped us in countless ways.

The Mill has let folks raise money for us there. It's also the place Marcus and I retreat to for a nice cold beer on a hot day when we need a break.

Hook And Cleaver was a local butcher that charged us almost nothing for an entire rib eye roast for our girls for Christmas dinner. OS Institute's owners allow our girls to have memberships there for no charge. They often check in on us to see what our needs may be.

Fuquay Family Dentistry showered us for Christmas this year with cash and gifts. They also help us with the dental needs of our girls. Biscuitville Restaurant included TWM in a benefit they did for a few non-profits.

One year, the Mason Jar Restaurant held one as well. Also Cross Towne Realty has supported us through my realtor friend and TWM donor, Diane Timony.

Let's talk about the Bob Barker Company. They "adopted" us a few years ago. They've supplied us with cleaning supplies and everything you could possibly need if you're a prisoner.

They are the largest supplier to prisons in the country. So, we have huge boxes full of toothpaste, razors, tampons, pads, toothbrushes, soap, laundry soap and anything else you can imagine. They've been incredible and we're so grateful. For Halloween one year, one of the girls dressed up in an orange prison jumpsuit and prison shoes to be an escaped convict!

I can't even begin to count and name the many individual folks that offer help, whether it be donations or rides for the girls or anything else that is needed.

People that I don't even know write me Facebook messages from the TWM Facebook and ask how they can help. They all say, "I love what you do!"

They compliment us and say all manner of kind things about how great they think we are. I so badly want to tell them that we're not great. Actually, we're a mess. But we're a happy mess! And we're trying.

4
Jessie

As a heroin addict chases a substance induced high, sex addicts are bingeing on chemicals. In this case, their own hormones.
- Alexandra Katehakis

She arrived at our home late one evening with her three year old son. Upon entering the living room, her son Max grabbed the first thing at his disposal, the remote control, and shattered it against the wall.

When she tried to correct him, he just yelled "f##k you!"

I knew we were in trouble.

Jessie was homeless and penniless. She and Max were a mess. We set them up in their room for the night. I went to bed shaking, wondering if I'd just made a huge mistake.

Jessie was a lovely girl with emotional problems that I tried and tried to understand. She had times of stability and real growth that would encourage us.

I fell in love with this girl easily. I began to see her as quite my own. She needed a lot of love. She and our daughter, Alex became close friends as well.

Each morning though, I'd find myself retreating to my room when I heard Max coming upstairs. There was something terribly wrong with him that my naïve eyes couldn't yet see, or maybe my mind couldn't yet comprehend.

"Max, please don't throw Marcus's books all over the floor."

"I will if I want!" or "I hate God!" would be his casual replies.

One time Marcus watched him for 20 minutes while Jessie and I went to the store. Max kept pulling his pants down and trying to show Marcus his back side.

He'd ask, "Want to see my butt?"

He would take his pants down and pee on a wall, or on the floor or all over the toilet seat. We would find it often by stepping in it.

There were times when Jessie and Max would be allowed to take Marcus's truck to run errands. What we found out later, is that she and Max were going to visit Max's father. Jessie would engage in violent sex with him while in the same room with Max.

Once Jessie told me about a time when Max was two, that she, Max and his father were in a motel room for a few nights.

Some "acquaintances" of Max's father came by for a while and offered to babysit Max. Jessie thought it was odd but went along with it. So, Jessie and Max's father left for an hour.

When they returned, when Jessie went to change Max's diaper, there was blood coming from his bottom. His own father had arranged for this to happen and Jessie knew it. But still, she kept taking Max to see him and engaging in sexual deviancy.

Jessie and Max lived with us at The Welcome Mission for a year or so when all of this came to light. I knew what I had to do. I had warned her that if she wouldn't protect Max, then I would! So, I called CPS.

I had Max taken away from Jessie that afternoon. It was one of the hardest things I've ever done, and I'd do it again if I ever have to, to protect a child.

Jessie knew what I had done. But I told her that I would help her get Max back if she changed her behavior, established some good boundaries and protected Max. She said she wanted that too.

She lived with us for almost nine more months, but she kept falling back again. Eventually she moved out. Max went to foster care for a few years before she finally did get him back.

I learned so much from Jessie and Max. God opened my eyes to atrocities that I couldn't even imagine and He also gave me compassion for victims of sexual abuse in a way I never had before. It was personal to me now.

My heart bleeds for Jessie. What is so broken in her that she would allow these things to happen to her son?

5
Sundays and Holidays

What is good is difficult, and what is difficult is rare.
- Robert Farrar Capon, *The Supper of the Lamb:*
A Culinary Reflection

There's a natural and nearly constant tension in my mind regarding the fact that this is our house and it has five bedrooms, and when I fill them with TWM girls, there is no room for my grown "birthed" kids and grandkids to come and visit.

I want everyone to be comfortable and for all to have a great time together. So, am I supposed to keep the rooms empty all the rest of the year, so my kids have a room when they visit? I always answer myself with "no".

These are issues that create real consternation in my mind, however. Will I have to put them in hotel rooms? How do I handle this and not let the girls know because it could make them feel badly? "Thanksgiving is a month away" I'd think to myself.

"So, maybe I don't bring someone new in the open room until after my birthed kids leave. Oh, but here's a girl that's about to be homeless, but you have to wait until after the holiday?"

No.

I've been making my family share their family holidays with people for many years now. For some of our girls, they've never had a real Christmas before!

It's always shocking to me when they buy a gift for some-one and attempt to give it to them weeks before Christmas because the actual day holds no special thought. So, Ma has a rule! No opening presents early!

So, I love to make Christmas special. For some, there's not been wrapped gifts under a tree in many years, if at all.

One year, we had the parents of one of our girls here for Christmas and some others here as well later that day for Christmas dinner. Fortunately, the weather was nice so we were able to set up tables and chairs out on the back patio.

We had the whole lovely picture! An outside fire place, the hanging lights, beautifully set tables with candles and greenery. I served Stuffed Beef Tenderloin, Twice Baked Potatoes and Asparagus with Hollandaise Sauce. I can't remember if I had homemade rolls or not. Likely not since I had the same crowd the night before for Christmas eve and was already exhausted.

There was a lot of laughter that day.

That's one of my favorite Christmas Welcome Mission memories.

There were many holidays years ago, where I wanted to just crawl into a hole until they were over. My family was torn apart. Relationships with my daughter and her husband were broken. I wasn't allowed to see the grandbaby that lived 20 minutes away.

I was in such despair. I think maybe one reason I love to do holidays up really big is because of those years. I know something about a lonely Christmas. I know something about wishing Christmas would just pass on by because it's too painful. Holidays shine a spotlight on broken families. They bring all the sadness right to the surface.

An excerpt from my journal from 12 years ago:

November 19, 2007:

"Thanksgiving is approaching. I still have no relationship with my daughter. It's been about a year now. I'm beginning to think I never will again. I can't take it. Please help me. Please help me. Help me get through the holiday. Sometimes the pain and anguish is unbearable."

I serve a God that loves to recycle our pain and use it for good.

Now, I no longer want to focus on what I have or what I'm missing. I want to make it less painful for others. I want to ease the suffering and loneliness for our girls.

I want them to experience the joy that comes from having people. Our people. My people. Your people. People that matter to us. We all want to feel a part of a group of people. Our tribe. I like to say that family isn't necessarily about blood.

I refuse to mourn what is or has been, but instead, make it better for someone else.

6
Two Years, Seven Months, Six Days

To love someone, is to show them their beauty, their worth and their importance
- Jean Vanier

A mutual acquaintance brought her to my house one night around 8:00 p.m.. She was pregnant and had nowhere to live. Within a little while we were alone on the couch just talking.

I knew God always seems to make it clear to me when I need Him to. And this was no exception. I knew she was the one He chose to move in. I had one room available.

My feelings on being pro-life have evolved throughout the years. Yes, life begins at conception, but I'm now more the "put up or shut up" kind of pro-lifer. We Christians need to do more than post on social media. We need to "take care of the orphan and the widow." (James 1:27).

Here I had before me, a single girl with an unborn child and they were in need.

Will we answer the call of Jesus on our lives? Is it easy? Absolutely not. All you need to be is willing. I am nothing special. I'm just willing.

Vanessa moved in on Valentines day, 2016.

Her earliest memories were of sexual abuse. Her mom was a stripper. Her father was and now is again, serving time in prison for sexual assault. Her childhood was not exactly pleasant. Sometimes they lived in a car.

When she went to school, there was one teacher that would sometimes tell her to take a shower and wash her hair in the locker room. Then the kind teacher would brush her hair.

This memory is one that means so much to Vanessa. Just the simple kindness of someone brushing her hair. Remember that when you don't think a small kindness can make a big difference in someone's life.

When she got older, she began sleeping around. This escalated to Craigslist, and casual hook-ups with strangers. Sometimes every single day. I've learned so much from Vanessa and her story. The unimaginable trauma she suffered as a child did something to her that brought her to this place of sex addiction.

It had a twisting effect on her that she can't totally even understand. I grew up with a very black and white view on these things. You're a bad person if you act this way.

You can't possibly love God if you act that way. I've come to see that not only can someone in this position love God, but even better, He can and does love them! The way I used to see it seems to run rampant in some church denominations or groups.

Ultimately, it comes back to how much better than you I am. We're always trying to seem better than others.

In 2014, she was kidnapped by a stranger she met for sex. She took him back to her home where he hogtied her and held her captive for hours. Some of us might be shocked at such dangerous behavior. Although saved several years earlier, she was running from God.

Her captor was caught and sent to prison and her dangerous behavior still continued. While running headlong from God as fast as she could, He stopped her with a brick wall.

She was pregnant.

Let me just pause here and repeat one of my lines I say to the girls, all the time, is that this is not a free hotel. God loves us where we are but we can't stay there.

There has to be growth to remain here at TWM. We're all on a journey. So, to live here, I have to see some growth of any sort, even baby steps, or I will ask them to leave. I can't walk for someone. I can only walk with them. I call it a hand-up, not a hand-out.

Vanessa moved in and she had great drive and determination to make a better life for her unborn baby. She was open about her addiction. She needed some help and accountability, and she needed love.

Most people are lacking love in their lives. They'll gravitate toward love and acceptance. We accepted Vanessa, even though her lifestyle had been so promiscuous. We accepted her because Christ accepts her. He died for her, so who are we to say who is or isn't worthy?

Vanessa ran full force toward the life that she knew God wanted for her. She knew that she couldn't stay where she was. She was broken sexually and she knew that Jesus would meet her at the well.

"Go and sin no more," He said. She didn't change in baby steps. She changed much faster than that. Sometimes well intentioned Christians don't walk away from their sin until they have help and discipleship along the way.

Baby K was born later that year in 2016. What a blessing this unplanned pregnancy was! They lived with us for over two years. We are now surrogate grandparents to baby K!

7
House Rules

*Behind flames and smoke atop Mount Sinai, God issued his
Ten Commandments to the wandering people of Israel.*
- as described in Exodus 19-20.

Here at TWM, we found we need 15 rules to cover
everything. The difference from Mount Sinai might be
that we are not desert nomads, and there are as many as
eight of us sharing a five-bedroom house.

If you're interested in some of the reasoning behind our
House Rules, please see the Rules chapter in Section II.

1. Church attendance on Sunday with the family

2. No taking the Lord's name as a curse word.

3. No sexual relations, on or off TWM property.

4. No drunkenness

5. No illegal drugs, used on or off TWM property

6. No pornography, including soft porn on TV shows

7. No dating (unless approved by Ma). No dating site accounts.

8. Obtain a job asap

9. Financial accountability with Ma and financial advisor to TWM

10. Basic hygiene observed, i.e. take a daily shower, brush teeth daily, wash hands after using the bathroom.

11. Wash hands when getting or making food.

12. 10:00 p.m. curfew so I can go to sleep (unless special circumstances arise)

13. Room kept clean. Bed made daily.

14. Kindness to one another, extending grace and mercy.

15. Do chores assigned by Ma.

8
And on Some Days We Struggle, Part I

Suffering can refine us rather than destroy us, because God himself walks with us in the fire.
- Timothy Keller

I'm lost. My heart is so greatly burdened after speaking with some others about Anne.

What if I do more to damage her by my ignorance? These thoughts make me want to get in my bed and stay there and not face it. Again, I feel so weak.

I love it when one of the girls tries to tell me how hard it is for them to live in someone else's house. They have no idea how hard this is for us.

I deal with constant complaining, when everything is provided for them, when I go to bed most nights so burdened for them and careful to measure each word I say.

They have no idea. So much jealousy and selfishness and it's exhausting. I retreat to my room often. Most days I have the strength to do it, but when I'm not feeling well, I just can't.

I feel like you have to be a robot to manage it all, but then someone needs me to be human, and I don't know how to switch.

9
Hope

I tell people, ya know, going to the club doesn't make you a bad person, and going to church doesn't make you a good one.
- Miley Cyrus

Hope came on a plane from California.

She'd been homeless, living on the streets for about a year and a half. Then she lived for about six months with an older man who was a Hell's Angel. She had been using all sorts of opioids and then ultimately, meth.

Her story begins when she was quite young. She was sexually abused by a neighbor for over a year. She tried telling her parents but she wasn't believed, so the abuse continued.

When her family moved to California, she was relieved to be free of the abuse and even as a young girl, she finally had hope for her future.

In her teenage years, her previous abuse began to take a toll on her and she started acting out sexually. She told her father that she needed help because she was freely "giving head" to boys she knew. But help didn't come. In fact, it was never spoken of again.

She ended up pregnant and so her father gave her and her boyfriend money to go to Vegas and get married.

After all, that's what good Christian families do. They get them married to hide the out of wedlock pregnancy. Hide the shame on the family.

She and her husband had three children together and the first few years were good, but then they began abusing prescription pain medicine. Her husband would often be passed out and unable to work. Many days, there was no food so Hope would have to go to local churches and food banks for food for the kids.

Finally, after a violent episode where her husband strangled her (that incident landed him in a mental institution), she asked her family if they would support her leaving him. They said they would. But what they actually did was take in her husband and her children instead. She was out.

This began her years on the streets.

Hope did a lot of things that she's not proud of. She abused drugs, she stole, and her life was out of control. And now, she was homeless. She wandered around for over a year, trying to survive. She ran from trafficking gangs, until she ended up with Marty.

Much older than Hope, Marty took her onto "the property" where he was staying in a filthy trailer that had no running water or electricity. There, she was controlled through abusive sex, drugs and daily beatings.

She used meth when he would give it to her. There was often no food, so she would wander the nearby town looking in dumpsters for food.

After some time on the property with Marty, she would get away to the library and get on her Facebook page, desperately seeking pictures of her precious children. I'd been seeing her unraveling for years through her posts. I'd known Hope for 15 years.

I sent her a private message in early 2016 that said "Come here. I just want to love on you."

She came to TWM late in the night, malnourished, exhausted and with brain fog from the meth use. Her first few minutes here at The Welcome Mission, she began searching for medicine.

"Where's the good medicine, Ma?" she said.

I was absolutely terrified. I grabbed every over the counter medicine we had and threw it in my bathroom while she wasn't watching! I finally got her settled down in her makeshift room we prepared for her in the basement (the other rooms were full) and drifted off to sleep myself.

The next morning, our daughter Alex was driving to work early when she called me from the driveway. I awoke from my deep sleep to Alex telling me, "Mom, I think Hope is sleeping on the neighbor's back porch!"

Sure enough, Hope had felt the need to guard their fire pit. Needless to say, our neighbors have been very patient with us.

For a long time, Hope didn't think clearly. Years of drug use had messed with her mind.

She wandered the streets of our town at night picking flowers from people's flower beds. I would fuss and tell her she cannot do that.

One day I woke up again to picked flowers and I said, "Hope! What did I say about picking people's flowers?" She replied, "It's ok Ma! I picked them from the Chamber of Commerce!"

That's our Hope. She told me her story over and over again. I'd listen and pray for her. I was in way over my head and not qualified for this.

I'd just listen and do my best to control her nightly movements. "Stay on TWM property!" I'd tell her to no avail. "Ok momma" she'd say. Then I'd wake up to random yard art she'd found or more flowers.

If she was awake during the day, she would be on the back porch smoking. I must have bought her two packs a day in those first weeks. People have questioned my judgment about her smoking cigarettes, but the way I saw it, it wasn't meth, so it was fine and temporary.

She had conversations with the birds and would relay to me what the conversations had been about. Then more tears. Then more stories. For days and days it went like that.

She hopped a bus and rode all the way back to California about a month after getting here. She thought Marty needed her. It took a few hours for her to let me know that had been a huge mistake. We flew her back here.

Over the two and a half years Hope lived here, the fog lifted and she began getting her life back. She never used meth again. Now she lives back in California and is reunited with her sweet kids.

If I did nothing else in my life but reunited Hope with her children, then I'm satisfied. That's good Jesus work, right there.

10
Non-Residents

For I know the plans I have for you," declares the Lord,
"Plans to prosper you and not to harm you, plans to give you
hope and a future
- Jeremiah 29:11

We've worked with and for many women that have never actually lived here at TWM. Most of my time is spent with non-residents either interviewing them over coffee, or counseling, or being there for someone that just needs a listening ear.

Some may need help renewing their driver's license, or taking the drivers test. We helped one woman in her 60's get her first drivers license in over ten years. We've given rides to doctor's appointments, taken food to someone that needed it, or given pregnancy test to a girl that thought she could be pregnant.

One girl I spent some time with was different. I don't know how to describe her, except that right off the bat, I noticed that her socialization skills seemed to be severely lacking with no appearance of a conscience. As time went on, it manifested in all sorts of ways from lying about her parents to turning people against people.

The best manipulators always use an element of truth to their lies. If the lies are too outlandish, they won't be believed.

But if they take the truth and twist it just enough to change the meaning, then the outcome can be very destructive.

This girl was a master. As is true of a narcissist, they use those clever lies to turn people against each other, so none of the people around them are speaking. That's when they can do the most harm.

If you know someone like this, pay attention to the people around them. Do they all, or (or at least many of them) mistrust and even possibly despise one another? If nobody is speaking to one another, then the narcissist can get away with all sorts of malicious acts. This is this girl's story and part of it played out here at TWM. She turned someone very special to us, against us, and in particular, me for over a year.

I really mourned that relationship. He was like a son to me and he was saved in my living room, on my couch a few years earlier. She successfully put a huge rift between him and all of us here at TWM.

After over a year, he showed up on my doorstep with a story. He didn't know if I would even talk to him. I hugged him immediately and then heard his story of pain and misery over the last year. My heart was so sad for him.

Thankfully, our relationship was restored but it doesn't always go that way.

There have been girls that stayed here for a night or two for various reasons. Some had a child, some didn't.

I've had girls come here for a few days to have someone to talk to because there were conflicts with their parents or boyfriends. They'd get good food, lots of conversation and especially love.

A girl busted into my house one day. She was having a full blown panic attack. She'd been drinking all night and felt like she couldn't breathe.

I called 911 and it seemed like the whole police force and EMS came screaming down the road.

It's not a new thing for the cops to come. Just another day in paradise at TWM. Another incident of the cops coming was when a girl that was here for lunch got mad at her son and went to the basement to spank him.

Apparently two things happened. One, she didn't just spank him, she wailed on him. Two, her phone in her back pocket butt-dialed 911. The whole thing was captured on a recording and the police responded.

Sweet Amy was one I spent a good deal of time with that didn't live here. She was this little ninety pound soaking wet, blond haired, blue eyed cutie that was 8 months pregnant when I met her. She also had a black eye. Her baby daddy was violent.

I talked to her for hours trying to get her away from him. She was also very hungry so I fed her often, when I could, and even had a baby shower for her so she would get the things she needed for her baby. Each time we met, I tried to get her to see that she was in danger. She didn't care. She wanted her man.

I woke up one morning to a text from a mutual friend that said "He killed her". I was so devastated! I immediately had to go drive over to her house. There was police tape everywhere. She was gone. I felt defeated.

I had a mutual friend with this other girl in Greensboro who was crying out for help. She'd tried to commit suicide before a few times and struggled a lot with depression and opioid addiction.

What's fascinating about this relationship I had with Jill, is that I never actually met her in person. We talked on the phone a lot and we messaged even more. If you've never presented the gospel over messenger, you haven't really dealt with this population of young adults.

It seems weird at first, but once you've done it time and-time again, it gets more "normal". Today's young adults want to communicate that way. It's their safe zone. So, go with it!

Jill and I talked for over a year. I'd be there for her when she needed a listening ear. I'd encourage her toward Jesus and love her in any way I could over the phone.

One day I was flipping through Facebook and saw that she had succeeded in her quest. She was gone. Another precious soul gone.

How do I keep going after these things happen? What the heck am I doing this for? These are my constant thoughts that plague me. I'm not good enough. I'm not strong enough. I cannot go on.

Yes to all of that. It's all true. Where I am weak, He is strong. He will carry me. I have more Amys and Jills out there. They need me and they need you.

11
Mary

It's messy. That doesn't mean it's a mistake. It's ministry.
- Unknown

There was this lady I was referred to who was married and had no children. She was probably about 10 years younger than I am, and I was told that she was very depressed.

A mutual friend, (a neighbor of hers), who I knew, asked me if I would spend some time with her and see if I could help her in some way. So I said sure. I called Mary and she agreed to go to lunch with me.

I took her to Chick-fil-A. I heard her story and about her struggles. There wasn't anything abnormal in the conversation. Just two people getting to know each other. There were no red flags.

After that lunch I took her back home and we planned to get together again. She did say she doesn't have a cell phone, so I couldn't text her. I had to call her landline and that seemed a little odd.

What grown woman doesn't have a cell phone? But I didn't ask for any explanation. It just was what it was. So the next week I went to pick her up again. She also didn't drive, (which in retrospect, was another odd thing).

I picked her up, and we went to Baskin Robbins. We sat and visited, had coffee. I could tell right away there was something odd about her, based on the things she said.

It's like she began to slowly open the door to her thoughts and what was going on with her to see how I would react. Well, it's not my first rodeo, so you know, with people with serious problems or things they've experienced in their lives.

I didn't react any way, I just was listening. So she opened the door a little bit more and she started telling me about a man that was stalking her.

At first I was horrified at the story she was telling me. But the more she talked, the more I raised an eyebrow and I thought, could this be true? Something doesn't seem to fit here. But she was very terrified of this man.

She never gave me his name, but she said the reason was that she doesn't use a cell phone. That was one of the reasons. So, now I'm starting to think, what is going on? She presented very put together.

She didn't seem, on the surface, to be off in any way. I just saw no red flags. But the more I got to know her and the more she talked, the more I started to doubt my original thoughts. So at this point, I had spent several times visiting her. I had her over to my home. She and her husband who worked at Fidelity Bank, came to our church.

And there just was a nagging suspicion in the back of my mind that there was some serious mental illness. But at the same time I would doubt myself and think, well, I don't know for sure. So I just kept spending time with her and being her friend.

She began to tell me that not only was this man stalking her, but she would come home from me picking her up for lunch and see that things were rearranged in her house.

She also began to tell me that there were pins, very small pins on the back of her furniture with a very, very, very thin wire that he had installed to spy on her in her house. I would ask her why he was spying on her and never really got an answer that made any sense.

I continued on. I thought she needed a friend, so I was going to be that person. So the next time I went to pick her up, we had been spending time together for about a month. She came out of her front door rolling a suitcase behind her. She opened my van back door, threw it in, got in the car, said, "let's go, hurry!"

I said, "Mary, where are we going?" She said, "we need to go to Staples. I need to make copies of something very important." I backed down her driveway and we headed to Staples. And along the way I'm thinking, what is going on here? So I asked her some more gentle questions. "So what exactly is in the suitcase, Mary?"

49

"It's documents! Documents that have come in the mail from the CIA," she said. Okay. My mind was blown. I repeated, "The CIA?"

She said "Yes, they've been watching me for a while. I've been getting mail from them, some of it disguised, some of it not. It's all in the suitcase is very very important that I make a copy of all of it because they are seeking to destroy this evidence."

We had to go Staples. We go into Staples with her dragging that suitcase and we get inside and I'm just trying to look into the suitcase. I want to see what is in that thing. She opens it up. She tells the manager she needs a copy made front and back of every single piece of paper in this suitcase. It was thousands of pieces of paper.

The manager looked at her and slowly said, "okay." She looked at me at that point, and honestly, I tried to pretend like I didn't know her! There was most definitely mental illness on board here.

Finally, I was able to sneak a peek into the suitcase and what I saw was basic everyday junk mail that you'd get in the mail from various stores like Kohl's or coupon books. It was all junk mail except I finally did see one real letter and it was handwritten to her with her address and in the top left hand corner of the return address was also her address. She sent a letter to herself and thought it was from the CIA.

At this point, all I could think of was, I gotta get out of here. This is so bizarre. Finally, the manager understands what she wants.

I'm thinking, how much is this going to cost? On the way to the car with the empty suitcase dragging behind her, she says to me, "I expect this building to be blown up or burned down tonight." Then she paused and stared at me. My eyes got huge!

At this point I actually became nervous about being with her. Obviously she had serious mental illness, schizophrenia, likely, I don't know, but she was so erratic and the things she was saying, I made an excuse to get out of lunch and I took her back home.

I only saw her one more time after that. She called me and said she was moving and would be leaving very soon. We said our goodbyes, and that's the last time I ever heard from Mary.

12
Be Careful What You Pray For

When it comes to serving those with a criminal record, I have yet to find one ministry that is more fruitful than our living rooms and dinner tables. If you aren't willing to have someone in your living room or at your dinner table...... what's the point?
- Pastor Jon Kelly

I felt really weary that day. I felt like God wasn't moving and that my efforts were useless (yes, there's a pattern here).

I prayed in the shower that morning that He would help my unbelief and do something extraordinary that day to help me see. I'm weak.

About a half hour later, I was walking into Harris Teeter and a woman stopped me to chat with me. She had seen me before with Theo and she wanted me to know that her son also has Down Syndrome.

She was very talkative and we ended up standing there for half an hour just chatting. Somehow she got my phone number and that began a several year odyssey that would shock me and ultimately frighten me.

In my work with TWM, I have attempted to be there for women in all sorts of circumstances. I've worked to serve married women in their trials as well.

She was someone on my radar that I felt needed friendship and help in some areas so I determined that I would be there for her.

She seemed lonely and wound tightly. She could talk a mile a minute and then grab you for a fast hug, say "love ya" and be gone in seconds. Some people you just naturally gravitate to.

She was never someone I would have sought out for meaningful, mutual friendship. We didn't have that natural connection. I wanted to be there for her nonetheless.

I invited them to our church and then to my house for the church potluck lunch. The whole family came. That day, I thought I'd lose my ever loving mind. The kids were just such a mess that my house was overrun. They fought, screamed and destroyed.

They stayed for hours. She never seemed to notice the chaos. I vowed I'd never do that again. I'm not that good!

I saw Leslie periodically for the next few years. Several times in Harris Teeter. I literally hid from her a few times if I saw her first. She was just too much for me. I know my limitations!

Then one day there was a knock on my door. We opened it to find Leslie on the ground wailing from a sprained ankle that just occurred on my front porch.

She had a homeless couple with her that she picked up off the street and brought them to my house. She brought them to my house to live!

After getting Leslie situated, I gave the couple some food and told them all that they cannot stay here. I knew absolutely nothing about them.

She took them home with her. That didn't go well at all. It turns out that they stayed for a long stretch of time and took great advantage of her kindness.

Throughout the time I knew her, there were strange illnesses, injuries, bankruptcies, GoFundMe pages set up by her, for her, and shared on social media again, and again, and again that nobody would donate to. I remember thinking that there has to be something wrong with her. But I couldn't pinpoint what it was. I just felt the need to run when I could.

I'd accidentally bump into her in random places like Walgreens. Then I'd be stuck for half an hour while she talked. Something was just not right. I just knew that I didn't want to be a part of whatever it was!

Then one day I saw on Facebook that Leslie had been bitten by a spider at work. Then a few days later, it wasn't a spider anymore, it was a tick after all and she came down with Lyme Disease. According to her, she was bedridden and dying.

She had EMS called to her house time and time and time again, until they would come but not take her anywhere. I would see this unfolding on social media. She would complain about all the medical professionals that wouldn't help her. She would get many "angry" emojis and comments which fueled her fervency.

Sometimes she would post recordings of phone calls with doctors that she was talking to and these recordings only showed all the more that something was not right.

One day last year, she asked me to come see her. She was desperate for someone to talk to from her bedside. UGH. I went because I felt that I needed to be kind to her. I felt guilty for all the thoughts I had had about her.

What if I was wrong? What if I'm still the judgmental person I used to be? I preach about having a heart for broken people. I was being a hypocrite! So, I went.

I had to walk past two dozen cats to get to her bedside. I did get the chance to pray with her and to encourage her in Christ. I brought her Ma's homemade lasagna for her family for supper as well. But what she really wanted was to prove to me that she had this disease. I think she could tell that I had begun to not believe her.

With me at her bedside, she called a doctor's office about her follow up. She put the phone on speaker phone. The nurse on the other end seemed very confused.

She said they had no record of Leslie ever going there or of any future appointment. Leslie pushed back, saying her records should have been sent there by now, but the nurse didn't know anything about it.

Now, I knew. I was convinced that she was either making it all up and lying, or that she had some mental disorder. I had no idea what to do. I ended up leaving soon after and that evening I called her husband and talked to him about it.

I was concerned for the whole family. He said that he believed her and that she wasn't making it up. At the end of the day, I decided that there was nothing more that I could do for her.

The "bedridden" Leslie showed up to my house several days later. She drove herself. She walked perfectly fine. Makeup on and hair done. She looked fine. She stood in my doorway and took a full hour to tell me, again, all the proof that she had Lyme Disease.

After an hour of this, I interrupted her and said, "I don't believe you. I think you made it up." She was shocked! So, she began again. So, I interrupted her again. "Leslie, I think you're lying." Her response blew me away. She said "What? Do you think I'm crazy? Do you think I'm going to bring a shotgun over here and blow everybody on this street up?"

I asked her to leave. I've not seen her since.

As someone that wants to help people, I often come across women that I'm not qualified to help. That's frustrating. It's also very discouraging because most days I think to myself, "What are you doing this for?"

13
Alyssa

A clear conscience is the sure sign of a bad memory.
- Mark Twain

She flew in from Spokane.

I picked her up from the airport around 10:00 p.m..

She was a tiny 20-year-old girl with a slight bump from her belly. I got her home and we sat for her to eat some homemade lasagna. She was all smiles but I had immediately noticed something odd about her.

Something in her didn't seem genuine. I see that a lot, actually with my girls. They don't know if they can trust you yet, or they don't trust anyone at all, or as in this girl, there was more.

She announced to me that night that she planned to have a home birth. As the Executive Director of TWM, I was a little startled since this was now her home! "Oh really?" I said.

"When you say 'home birth' do you mean *at home,* as in here at TWM?"

"Oh YES!" she exclaimed. Needless to say, I let her know in no uncertain terms that she would absolutely not be giving birth at TWM but instead in a hospital.

Our first night got off to a rocky start because she was angry. It's really difficult to bring someone in to your home to live and provide for their every need, only for them to get angry because you aren't serving them the way they want to be served.

Imagine doing something for someone that sacrifices not only you but also your time and relationship with your husband and children, and that person spits in your face because you did it wrong.

That's the best way to describe the situation I was in with this girl and some others as well. It also describes quite well how I respond to God when He doesn't do what I want or think is best for my life.

Sometimes I don't like how He sent his Son to die for me and then doesn't see the value of my decisions! It makes no sense at all when it's turned around on me. So, I remind myself of this fact very frequently, which helps me be patient and merciful.

However, Alyssa made progress somewhat through the rest of her pregnancy. She did her chores and most of the time she had a good attitude. Until she didn't.

There were times where she would seem to lose her mind and turn into another person altogether. Tantrums, crying, throwing things, slamming doors, screaming vulgarities at me and everyone else.

She would smack her belly screaming that she hated "it'". She screamed that she didn't want "it". That "it" had ruined her life. Lord have mercy.

Those were hard days. She would get over those tantrums and apologize and then we'd go on to another day!

The day of delivery came. We all went to the hospital. She wanted me there for his birth. She was adamant however, that nobody was allowed to hold her baby though. Nobody. Not even Ma.

Alyssa was living at this point down the street in our second house with her newborn baby boy, so it took me a little while to realize that not every mother has motherly intuition.

This new mother had none. She tried to care for her baby but she didn't seem to actually love her baby but seemed to be faking love. I would shake my head and think that I'm being paranoid. But it kept happening.

One day it occurred to me that the baby was too thin. I talked to Alyssa about it and she admitted that she didn't want him to be fat so she wasn't feeding him too much.

So, that's when I moved her back to the main house so I could better monitor her. I made her write on the whiteboard each feeding time and how many ounces she gave him.

Within a few weeks of being back at the main house, her ability to fake her affection for this baby became impossible. Her detached attitude toward him was something to see. It was mind-boggling. I didn't understand it. And it scared me. I began to become afraid for him.

Then, a few of the other girls heard her plop the baby down and yell at him to "Shut the f$%@ up!" That night I feared that the baby wouldn't be alive when we woke up the next day.

I sent someone to the courthouse to have her involuntary committed for evaluation. The police arrived about an hour later. They handcuffed her and took her to the hospital. It's kind of shocking how easy it is to do that.

She was released a few days later to the homeless shelter in Raleigh. I did meet with her to evaluate if she could return to TWM. I considered it very seriously.

However, our board wisely stepped in and advised me against it because Alyssa was so volatile toward me. They were right. She saw me as the person that took her baby away. Even though that's true in one sense, she fails to recognize that it was her behavior that brought me to that place.

I have absolutely no pleasure in doing something like that. In fact, it terrifies me, messing with people's lives like that.

I'd better be right because these actions of mine had huge ramifications and I knew that. That's one reason why I rely so heavily on the help and advice of our board members.

I have not seen her since, but I have heard some of her thoughts about me on social media. I won't repeat them. I look back on her with sadness because Alyssa is psychologically broken in ways I don't understand. She moves from man to man. She seems to have no conscience or sorrow. She seems to be lacking in emotion altogether.

Her baby was adopted by a wonderful family and is thriving. I look back at the eight months Alyssa lived here, as a victory for her child. They were very hard for us. But it was worth it.

14
And on Some Days We Struggle, Part II

In the crushing, you are making new wine.
- Hillsong Worship

Journal Entry:
The overwhelming sense of doom and potential loss of these girls overtakes me sometimes. I know the outcome is to God, but the part that I'm supposed to be, I fear I'm failing all the time. I need to spend more time with them individually...but I'm just trying to keep my head above water.

Anne is so hard. Twisted family life. Her heart is so broken and torn. Alcohol is her best friend. It's all she seems to think about. Numbing. Escaping pain. How can I get mad at her? But sometimes I do. So frustrating. She tries to convince me that Hope is faking it. She makes me wonder. Defeated. Some days I feel like this is all for nothing.

One of the hardest things about this work is when a girl goes hostile on me. Her whole heart and attitude is changed for one reason or another. There are often different levels of hostile experienced here.

One end of the spectrum is just not engaged anymore with me or the other girls. Reclusive. The other end of the spectrum is out right cussing me out and slamming doors. Both suck. Both hurt.

Preparing for Joy to come. Nervous. I always feel this way before a new girl arrives. Questioning myself. Hope and Vanessa are doing better. There always seems to be some conflict or drama. Something for me to sort out. Someone ends up angry.

15
Jan

When you smoke the herb, it reveals you to yourself
- Bob Marley

A mutual friend let me know Jan's location: the hospital. Her seventh abortion was scheduled for Tuesday.

I got to the hospital as soon as I possibly could, praying all the way that she would agree to give me a shot at helping her get through the pregnancy. She told me that she had hyperemesis and once she reached 20-something weeks, she could no longer keep going because her body would begin to shut down.

Jesus help me! When I arrived, I saw Jan dry heaving into a bed pan. She was a mess: weeping, begging for help, dry-heaving, repeat.

Then she jumped up and wanted me to follow her out of her room! In her hospital gown, which was open to the back, her hand attempting to keep the material together. In her bare feet, she grabbed her purse and off we went to the elevator. It finally dawned on me where we were going. She had to smoke.

Jan was all over the place emotionally, crying one minute and laughing the next. She smoked in the courtyard amidst all the "No Smoking" signs.

Countless people were walking by, staring at this girl with the pink hair, in the hospital gown, periodically throwing up in the shrubbery, with a cigarette hanging out of her mouth.

"Come home with me" I said to her. "Let me help you."

Even as I said the words, I thought, "Are you crazy, Holly?"

Jan came home with me that day. It began the toughest six months of our ministry. Those six months took me to the brink of insanity. Everyone in the house came close to losing our minds.

I truly believed that if she had regular, healthy meals, accompanied with lots of love and care, that I could help her keep her baby.

"Her problem is that her life is so crazy and out of control" I'd tell myself.

"She just needs Jesus" I'd think to myself.

Jan didn't have hyperemesis. She had an opiate addiction. My eyes weren't open to the real problem. I was still a novice.

Jan began to make progress. She stopped throwing up and began to get color back into her cheeks.

It was working: the good food, the hard work, a comfortable, stable home and all the love was healing her. Her baby was going to live and all would be well. I was naïve, remember?

Jan developed severe tooth pain. She had to see a dentist.

"Who is your dentist, Ma? I'd like you to take me to the one you see!"

I set up an appointment for her to see my dentist and I dropped her off there and planned for someone else to pick her up after her appointment.

She came home later that day feeling so much better. The dentist had given her some pain meds, because he said he'd rather she take those over Tylenol, for the baby's sake. That was a Tuesday.

By Sunday, the severe throwing up had returned. Jan was downing every liquid that she could find in the house and throwing it up within seconds of drinking it. She would bound loudly into the kitchen, find liquid - any liquid, down it and then run to her room to throw it back up.

We put an orange five-gallon bucket in her room, beside her bed for her to vomit into. She threw up in my yard, in the shower, on the floor, on walls, and pretty much everywhere.

I had no idea why the hyperemesis had returned. She had been doing so well! Concerned for the baby, I took Jan back to the emergency room and dropped her off, so I could go back to the house to clean up.

I came home to a disaster. It was worse than I could have ever imagined in her room. I entered and saw that the orange five gallon bucket was overflowing with vomit.

It was overflowing, all over the wood floor. Her bed had vomit all over it! Some was fresh, some was days old and dried. It was even dripping down her mattress.

What in the world?

As we began to clean it up, I noticed three empty prescription bottles scattered about. I picked them up, one by one and placed them on the bedside table. They were for Percocet and each script was for 30 pills.

All 90 pills were gone. They had been prescribed to her five days earlier. She had convinced the dentist to give her more than the original 30 tablets.

I was horrified. No wonder she was acting so irrationally and out of her mind: 90 Percocet tablets in four days!

The emergency room released Jan the next day. I picked her up and took her to the OB-GYN to see if the baby was ok. I took her to a renowned physician that I respected.

He looked at her and said, "She's in withdrawal."Now, I began to understand. She would take enormous amounts of pills, then go through withdrawal when she ran out.

After we got home I began to look through her Facebook page as well and going back about three years. There were countless tooth pain events.

My heart sank more and more. I'd been duped. My hopes and dreams for Jan and for her baby came crashing down. She needed more than I was able to do to help her. Nonetheless, we kept on.

What option did I have?

She would threaten to abort this child as she had the others if I made her leave. She'd already had a few late term abortions so I believed her. I was determined to see this baby born, but oh Jesus, how would she withstand this onslaught of narcotics on her tiny body?

Jan chain-smoked and was often emotionally and verbally abusive to me and others in the house. We had to search her things on occasion looking for any medication or illegal drugs. I caught her smoking pot in the front yard one night out of a cored out apple.

Night times were the worst. I couldn't sleep much. Jan would wander the house, lumbering down the hallway, and take shower after shower after shower.

The showers helped her feel better when she was nauseous. No soap was ever used, mind you. Just hot, steamy, vomit smelling, water all over the floor, showers.

One night, Marcus had had enough. He turned the hot water off from the valve in the basement, in the middle of her shower. She came bounding into our room minutes later, soaking wet, in a towel, complaining that our water had been shut off. We just said "ok". After she left, we chuckled quite a bit.

Her baby girl was born a few long months later. She was healthy and perfect. What the long term effects are on her, is yet to be seen.

As I held her for the first time, I wept. She was alive! She has a chance to live her life! What would that life be like, I didn't know. I prayed over her for God to use her life as a testimony to Him.

I heard from Jan a few weeks ago. She wanted to let me know how much she hated me. She took about 25 long, vulgar, nasty, text messages to tell me how she wished she had aborted her child. I believe Jan has some undiagnosed mental illness. This story makes me sad and it makes me shiver. These were by far, the hardest months we have ever experienced with TWM.

The good news is that her daughter has been adopted by wonderful people and I've been told she is thriving in their care. She's taking dance classes and playing soccer.

16
You're More Valuable Than That

I praise you because I am fearfully and wonderfully made.
- Psalm 139:14

She was referred to me by a friend in Fuquay-Varina. She was crying and a mess and needed me to come talk to her. So I did. Her story was one of a lot of abuse by her child's father.

You know, people that haven't ever been abused by a significant other tend to ask why they don't just leave? It's actually a lot more complicated than that.

There's emotional attachment, there's emotional abuse that thwarts the woman's thinking, and there are often children to think of and how to make sure they stay with you. And there are all sorts of roadblocks. One of the biggest ones is, where will I go? How will I support myself and my child (or children)?

So, often girls stay because they have no choice. There's one more reason the church needs to be a haven of refuge for women in these situations.

What if we had choices to offer them? What if we established The Presbyterian Safe House, or the First Baptist Safe House for Women?

Remember a time when denominations built hospitals?

Churches used to rescue orphaned children too. Now, we seem to fight amongst ourselves about stupid stuff like if the church should have a nursery during worship, or whether or not we should sing hymns or praise music. Good grief! There's work to be done.

Our pastor once said, "That's not a hill I'm willing to die on." So, the hills that aren't worth going to battle over need to be set aside so the church can do good works again.

One of my favorite things is to help a woman find her voice. Once she begins to see that she does have options, she begins to see herself differently.

I repeat the same mantra each time, "you're more valuable than that. You're worth more than this. Do not let him control you like that. You aren't those things that he calls you when he's angry! You aren't a piece of trash. You're made in God's image and he loves you."

Tammy needed help getting her child and her things from their house that she shared with her abuser. So, late that night, we, along with a sheriff's deputy, went to the residence for her to gather her things and her daughter.

There were guns everywhere and neo-Nazi paraphernalia. He was a gang member. He was a member of a dangerous neo-Nazi gang. This presented a problem for me having her at TWM. It's our home.

I had a responsibility not only to my family, but also the other girls that lived here for safety.

We try to keep a certain level of anonymity here. We don't have a sign outside that says this is TWM for this very reason.

My biggest problem was that I really loved this girl and her child. I really badly wanted them to stay here.

I took it to our board for counsel. The board agreed with me that it was too dangerous. The abuser was searching all over town for her. One day while I was reading in The Mill, I saw him burst through the door, evidently he was searching for her. I sank in my seat and hid my face with my book.

Eventually, he would find her. So, after a few days, I had to tell her that she had to go and that I would take her to Interact, a safe house for abused women. They had the capability to keep her safe.

It was gut wrenching for me.

She did eventually go back to him. She stayed with him for a few more years and then the abuse got to be too much for her again and she left. She's in a safe place now and I believe she won't go back.

These stories are so hard. Girls go back to abusers several times before they get free.

I want them all to know that they're more valuable than that. They're worth more than this. I want to do more for women in abusive relationships. Let's band together and make a difference for them!

17
Parents

If we know exactly where we're going, exactly how to get there, and exactly what we'll see along the way, we won't learn anything.
- Scott Peck, *People of the Lie*

One of the most difficult parts of this work is how to handle some of the parents of the girls. It can be difficult for a few reasons. The first being, I was, and am, one of them. I have a daughter in much the same scenario as they do. I have run the whole gamut of emotions, struggles and bad choices.

I've obsessed over my prodigal. I've lashed out in anger over her. I've enabled her. I've hurt her, loved her, cared for her, and even cut her off before.

On the one hand, I don't ever want to judge them for how they've handled their daughter. It's frustrating and heart breaking.

At the end of the day, I do get frustrated with parents that don't (or won't) do the best for their kids, when the kid is really trying to change their life.

We can never give up on them! Especially if she has turned away from her previous bad choices. Some days, giving up sounds so wonderful and peaceful. But nothing really good ever comes easily.

That's not to say that sometimes the best course of action for their grown kid, may be backing out of their life. Parents can be such enablers, and also sometimes we need boundaries of our own. But being unkind and kicking them while they're down and reaching up, is uncalled for.

I cannot even begin to count the hours I've spent counseling parents either over the phone, over text or messenger. I email updates when I can and encourage them with any baby step I see. But it doesn't always end well.

I end up taking the brunt of it when things go awry. I'm sure I've failed them in many ways but it hurts because I was at least willing. I tried to help. I stuck my neck out there.

One mother showed up here to my house very intoxicated and I simply asked her to not ever do that again. She wrote me a message and unleashed bitter, nasty hatred toward me that put me in bed for 24 hours. It cut me to the core.

Another called me and proceeded to call me every name in the book. I cried myself to sleep that night.

Both of those moms ended up apologizing to me later. I certainly accepted those apologies! But at the time they happened, I think the reason it wounded me so, is because there was some truth there.

When I get called a hypocrite (and I do often), I take it to heart because it's true. Maybe not the way they meant it, but I am one, as is everyone to a degree or another. That's why it wounds me and depresses me. They're right. Time for more humbling and repentance for me. UGH!

It's so hard to grow! I keep building up my pedestal and Jesus keeps knocking it down. He wants my undivided allegiance, and he deserves it.

Many of these parents became my friends, people I cared about. People I had here for Christmas and other holidays. Many have walked away from me because the end result wasn't what they expected or wanted, or they just don't need my services any more. It hurts.

I opened my heart and my home and often even forced my older children to share holidays with these folks when they came to visit from out of state. One Christmas we had 25 people here for Christmas day and dinner. It was a lot of fun, hard work and great fellowship.

If a girl is forced to leave because of her continued lack of respect for the rules of the house, then they go home and talk about us. They tell lies about me. More friends lost. More people walk away.

This has happened often. I'm not sure people realize just how lonely this work can be at times. When you open your heart (and you have to if you want to actually love people), you set yourself up for pain. Love is risky.

I got a hard copy letter from the father of one of the girls here who had been doing well here for six months. It was angry, threatening and very hurtful. He didn't appreciate the direction I'd taken with his daughter and wanted to make sure I understood his wrath, which is so interesting when I am the one housing, feeding and caring for his adult child for him.

I never answered it, but I prayed about it and for him. It hurt me deeply. I still have it. I only read it once until today, while writing this book. He is mean spirited, unloving, unforgiving and his words rang hollow and untrue. I'm sure he thinks he "won" because I never answered it and we didn't go forward with our intentions, but all he did was hurt his daughter again. There's no winner there.

Another thing I've observed in many parents, is that if their daughter does well here, they sometimes get jealous. That jealousy presents itself in many different ways. Sometimes it's in anger toward me and sometimes it's indifference but now, I tell the parents upfront to expect those feelings. I understand it! I probably would too. But I try to head it off in the beginning now.

Why keep doing it?

I do it because it's Jesus' call on my life. I do it because I can't not do it. It gives me a reason to live. It gives me purpose. And if I can help only ONE girl then it's all worth it. That ONE girl has been changed and for generations to follow, there will be better lives for it.

78

18
Anne

To love is not just to do something for them but to reveal to them their own uniqueness, to tell them that they are special and worthy of attention.
- Jean Vanier

The day I met this girl, I knew I wanted her to live with us. She was socially awkward, had pink hair and drawings all over her arms and her eyes constantly on her tablet that she used for communication with her girlfriend.

She would be the first to tell you that she had a lot of problems. The attempt to hide the cut marks on her arms with a long sleeve shirt in the hot summer, also drew me to her. These are the girls that melt my heart. The ones that just need a lot of love and care.

I saw her around our town a few times over the next year or so. We began to develop a friendship. She began opening up to me and once she did, she talked and talked and talked. Eventually, she needed a place to live. I was poised and ready. I'd been praying for her for a long time already, and so had our board members.

I think it was the very first full day here that she did one of her drawings on another girl's leg. She worked on that picture for a long time and nobody bothered to watch her as she drew it. Once she was finished, she was excited for her masterpiece to be shown.

The picture took my breath away when I looked at it. It was a phallic symbol in the mouth of a clown, and it was detailed. She's actually a great artist.

Ma had to make a new rule for Anne. No more penises. How I hoped we could get that washed off in time for church the next day, or the girl would be wearing pants for sure.

Anne had a hard time keeping still. It was never so obvious as when we were in church. So, she brought her markers with her and drew all over herself and others during church the next day. I was praying it wouldn't be a penis. I was relieved to see she drew flowers.

Anne and I have been through a lot together over the years. I love her and I know she loves me. She only stayed at TWM for about six months. She's got some demons she's dealing with and had some difficulty keeping a few of the rules. Like the time she snuck a friend (a guy) in through her bedroom window.

A mutual friend told me she had done it, but I couldn't rat out the friend, so I told Anne that I saw the guy on the surveillance tape sneaking in. The look on her face was priceless when she was thinking about how that could have been since there's no camera to her knowledge on that side of the house.

I was in Texas, visiting my mom and dad when I got the call that Anne had broken the rules again.

She wasn't going forward at all. In fact, she was going backwards. I had to tell her it was time to go. That was one of the hardest things I've had to do.

It makes me cry to tell it. She is a special girl. We still have a relationship to this day. She comes over to TWM when she needs something or when she just wants to visit.

She's one that I worry the most about damaging further. Did I help her? Maybe for a time. I spent countless hours talking with her on the back porch. Sometimes I feel like I'm just spinning my wheels.

It's so hard to pour your heart into someone and to love them with your entire heart and then feel like you did it wrong or weren't effective for some reason.

I remind myself that people with the problems on this level had a lifetime to make and a few months aren't going to reverse the effects of that.

I want to see her doing well! I want to see her happy and growing! I want to see her chasing after Jesus and loving herself enough to take care of herself!

I often feel like we take a few steps forward and more steps backward in this work. I must repeat Galatians 6:9 to myself all the time, "And let us not grow weary while doing good, for in due season we shall reap, if we do not lose heart."

If we do not lose heart...Do not lose heart...Stay the course that's before me...Do not grow weary...Hold on to what you know is right and true...Never let naysayers or critics make you swerve to the left or the right... Stay focused on the goal, which is Christ Jesus and through him, show his love to my neighbors and planting seeds.

Keith Green has a song called "I Want To Be More Like Jesus" where he talks about being blind to other's needs and tired of planting seeds. I can relate to those words on many days.

And the waves of adversity keep coming. They come one after the other and some of them are huge and they knock me down. But, I know I have to get back up and keep going.

Anne still needs me.

Postscript: Anne is back at TWM and doing so well! My heart is beaming with joy.

19
Meetings at The Mill

Sometimes it's ok if the only thing you did today was drink coffee.
- Sign at The Mill

I love my Diet Coke, but coffee is the great equalizer.

I met a girl for coffee one day that had called me asking for help. She got my number off of the website.

I often meet people at The Mill, here in Fuquay, instead of bringing them straight to the house. First, I need to know if I can even give them our address.

I met Shameka for coffee. She had this pissed-off look on her face. I didn't know who she was angry at but I decided maybe she was just hurting or sad.

I pressed on. I asked her my typical questions about her life. Often, girls will tell me things I need to know to make a decision about whether or not they are a candidate to move in. I can help anybody but not just anyone can move in, because of safety reasons.

The girls and their stories are my favorite part of this work. People's lives are fascinating to me. These girls are in these situations because of traumatic things in their lives.

83

Inevitably there will be pain in their eyes as they talk. If you know how to ask the right questions and know how to listen, you can learn a lot.

Another thing I've learned along the way is how to sit when having these conversations. If you sit slouched back, you're portraying an attitude of indifference. You must not care. If you sit arms crossed leaning forward, that's too aggressive. So, I'm always thinking about my posture when I meet someone.

Lastly, I try to remember to just listen. So many young women and men have come to talk to me simply because I listen to them. This young generation doesn't have anyone to listen to their cares, concerns and thoughts. I'm not there at the first meeting to offer advice. I'm there to listen, ask questions and determine what kind of help I can provide.

There is one (and one only) reason that I cannot help someone, and that is if they lie to me. I tell them that I don't care what you've done or where you've been, that I want to help but I can't help without the truth. If they lie to me, and I catch them in that lie, I will confront it and ask them for the truth.

If they're unwilling to tell the truth, I have to walk away. I've been lied to about current or past drug use, about boyfriends, about girlfriends, about sneaking someone into their room, about parents, about most anything.

I met Shameka for coffee. One of my questions was, "Have you ever been charged with a felony?" I always remind them that this does NOT mean I won't help them. I've had convicted felons live at TWM. She hesitated just a split second, and said, "no." I knew it meant yes. So, I asked her again and again she said, "no."

I went home and did a little social media checking and that led me to her mugshot. Her charge was "Abuse to a disabled person". My heart skipped a beat.

I confronted her on the lie and she got angry. I never heard from her again.

20
Kat

Experiencing pain over our children
is a part of image-bearing. God weeps too.
-Jack Fennema

I flew to Idaho for the birth. It was important for me to be there. As I sat in that hospital room watching her going through labor, I wondered to myself, why this didn't make me emotional?

Why wasn't I crying tears of sorrow for her pain? Or tears of sadness at the spectacle I was observing? Or tears of joy at the impending birth of this precious little boy? I sat there with a blank stare.

"Have you used drugs or alcohol during your pregnancy?" The nurse asked.

"No, of course not!" Kat retorted incredulously.

As the nurse left the room, Kat and her friend both snickered. I knew she had used pretty much anything and everything. I saw some of it the night before! And I had to wonder as the baby's vitals wavered to a frightening place, was she to blame for this?

She has spent the larger portion of her adulthood on various means to get high. It began, I believe with alcohol.

86

She's one of those rare people that doesn't really have a traumatic event or story that brought her to this place. She did have a controlling mother when she was growing up. I do have to wonder how much that helped her get to where she is now.

She got married and had two kids. The kids were well loved and cared for at first but her ever increasing drinking turned into daily binging. The desire to shirk off responsibilities in favor of fun became her daily choice. Watching this happen was altogether very sad and also quite confusing.

You see, Kat is a master manipulator. She could make you believe anything, especially if you really wanted to believe it. Her wrath and fury, if you dared question her was extraordinary and terrifying.

She had a way of controlling the people that loved her through lies. She was especially adept at "divide and conquer." She worked very hard at turning people against one another, so she could achieve her goals, whatever they were.

Kat is my first born child.

Kat was my training ground for The Welcome Mission. It was, and still is, the most grueling and heartbreaking training.

Kat is an addict.

87

She often reminds me that I shouldn't be able to sleep at night, helping all these girls here and not willing to help her. She has labeled me a hypocrite. I accept that name, to an extent, but not the way she means it. You see, I have helped Kat for 34 years. I've been her chief enabler for so long. I had to finally begin to say "no more."

When she was in her early and mid 20's, her lies and constant cruelty toward me would often land me in the bed for days, unable to function. The pain was worse than a death, because it was a constant sore with a nasty, puss-filled scab that was being ripped off again and again, so there's never healing. My journal from those horrid years shows such desperation from a broken mother.

July 19th, 2007
"I am just in such despair over Kat. I don't know how to handle it. She doesn't care about me any more and nothing I do will get through to her. Since Christmas, it has been a living hell. I feel as though I'm going crazy most days. You can't make someone love you."

In my despair, I contemplated suicide more times than I'd like to count. I turned to alcohol to numb the pain.

She manipulated everyone such that we couldn't even see our own grandchildren, who lived 20 minutes away.

My heart was constantly ripped out. I cannot even find the words to express the depth of my sadness for those years.

As I sit here right now writing this book in 2019 about my life and ministry, I'm still in the midst of utter turmoil over my daughter. She is a meth addict and is basically homeless. Oh she finds places to stay temporarily, but she has no home of her own. She has no car. She has no job, other than dealing drugs.

Meth is her first love. I know she has some feelings of love for her children, but she has pulled them through the mud with her, putting them in horrendous and dangerous situations. It's not fair to them. It's not right. They've been the ones to pay the highest cost of her addictions.

It's a terrible thing to be the mother of an addict. One minute she's nice to me because she wants money. The next minute she is so hateful that she manages to rip my heart out again. Whatever terrible words you can think of, she has called me them.

Her anger toward me is usually the result of me speaking truth to her. She rips me to shreds. There are days when I think it would be great to never see or hear from her again. Just being honest. It's the days that I do have feelings for her that do me in.

Those are bad days for me. If I feel, I hurt. So, it's easier to keep the walls up. Put her out of my mind (as best I can) and move on to help someone else because I cannot help her.

I know some may criticize me for writing about this. That's ok. I think it's better to talk about painful things, even private ones, because it can help someone else. I believe that God recycles tears.

If my pain can help someone else not feel so alone, or encourage someone to use it for good in others lives, then it's worth it to shed the light of day on it.

She's one of the main reasons my heart is drawn toward girls in trouble. Kat is a beautiful, gregarious, charming and gifted young woman. She could accomplish so much. But right now, she is like a shell of a person.

I flew to Idaho where she lives and saw her several months ago. It had been about two years since I last saw her. The changes were unbelievable. There were no Instagram filters available for this real life encounter.

It was just Kat, as she appears now and her broken mother, face to face. I couldn't stop touching her. I couldn't keep my hands off of her, as if somehow I could heal her.

Tears were streaming down my face as I looked at this pitiful sight. I felt no malice for all the years of hatefulness. I felt only sadness and pity.

I cannot help her. I'm a sucker for her and she would manipulate me to get what she wants. I need someone else to speak truth to her. I need someone else to have a Welcome Mission where she can get well, when she's ready.

We need Welcome Missions all over the place for women and men to get well. I need people to love her with truth and a hand-up and out of the cesspool where she resides.

She can't hear me. But she (and others) might be able to hear you.

21
And on Some Days We Struggle, Part III

Lord, hear my prayer.
Listen to my cry for help.
-Psalm 102:1

I don't know what to do right now, other than get in my bed. I keep telling myself to do the next thing. Making someone leave because they lied and brought drugs into the house sounds cut and dried.

The reality is, this girl has nowhere to go and it's breaking my heart for her to keep leaving me voicemails, begging me to stay. If it were just me here, I might be willing to try again. But I have to keep my son and everyone else safe with my decisions. I no longer trust her.

One way to know there have been drugs in the house is when you pack someone's stuff all up and find random strange things, like a Mountain Dew bottle with some weird looking foreign liquid in it that smells disgusting.

Or, random trash in odd places and a level of untidiness that goes along with the whole thing. A dropped (special) gummy bear, or random empty pill bottles and over the counter meds strewn about. It's the picture of sadness.

An addict will search for any way to get high.

When you decide that enough is enough, you're the enemy. All wrath turns against you. You aren't serving them like they want to be served, which is letting them do whatever they want, with no consequences.

But that's not love. At least, that's what I keep telling myself.

Love has boundaries. Boundaries for both you and for them. It's not love to let her stay and destroy herself and everyone around her.

Love meant calling the police to come and get her. Love meant not retaliating when she realized what's happening and lashed out with hateful words.

Love may mean letting her hit rock bottom, knowing that she could die in the process. So, my heart hurts today. I think I will go to bed.

22
Amy Carmichael

Don't bother to give God instructions, just report for duty.
- Corrie Ten Boom

Amy Carmichael was a young missionary in India in the late 1800's. She spent fifty-three years there, rescuing orphaned children from the temples, where they were used for temple prostitution. I read a book several years ago by Elizabeth Elliot called *A Chance To Die*. It's the incredible story of Amy's life.

She is the main source of my inspiration.

Prior to her ministry in India, as a young girl, she saw the suffering of the poor women where she lived in Millisle, Ireland. As Elisabeth Elliot puts it in *A Chance To Die*, "Her powers of observation were exquisite, her sympathy boundless, even as we will see later, for creatures the rest of the world thinks worthy of nothing but death." She saw the poor. She saw their suffering.

Amy would wander, as a young girl, into the slums to gather women for weekly prayer meeting. The good and proper people of her church weren't all too happy to have people of such low estate brought to their services. So, money was raised and eventually, Amy was able to purchase a slice of land. Someone donated the money to build a building as well.

One of my favorite things she's written and quoted by El-liot was "So you see, after all, cruelty and wrong are not the greatest forces in the world. There is nothing eternal in them. Only love is eternal."

In 2015, when we decided that after all these years of serving our girls, we should begin an actual non-profit. Our first step was what to call it? It was easy for me. I wanted it to be "The Welcome."

Marcus thought that it needed "Mission" in the name, so that people would get an idea what we're about. I agreed to the addition. The Welcome Mission was born.

When Amy was in India for all those years, she rescued over seven hundred children from temple prostitution. She was known to them as "Amma" which is "Mother" in Indian. She had many more kids than I will ever have.

On those days when I'm weary or exhausted, I like to remind myself of this remarkable woman and it inspires me to keep going. The orphanage she began in India is still there today.

One day, I will visit there.

I hope God gives me many more years to serve our girls. We have hopes and dreams of TWM graduates (or others) continuing our work when we're gone. We have dreams of a larger property were we can take in more women at a time.

I also dream of our girls, coming "home" to TWM and it being beautiful, because often times, our girls don't believe they're deserving of anything beautiful. That would be the first example of God's love for them, a beautiful place to call home. But it requires money. We need money to continue our work and a lot of money to expand it.

One of my about-to-be homeless girls initially had to stay in our basement bedroom. It's dark and cold and not very welcoming but that was the only room available.

We fixed it up as best as we could and moved her in on a Sunday. I apologized for the "dungeon" room we provided for her. I thought she deserved so much more. Her response was priceless. "It's a castle to me."

23
Daddy Issues

There is nothing that moves a loving father's soul quite like his child's cry.
- Joni Eareckson Tada

Most girls that come here to TWM have either had no father, or their father was not a great father.

One of the reasons this ministry works so well for us and our marriage is because Marcus isn't touchy-feely. He has boundaries. He's not wanting to be someone's confidant. He doesn't even want to hug anyone but me or his family.

I've often thought about how perfect he is for this behind-the-scenes work. He loves me passionately. He's utterly devoted to me and he doesn't make me feel insecure with young women all around the house all the time.

I'm keenly aware of the fact that I'm 54 years old. I'm about 100 pounds more than when he and I met 36 years ago, and I'm fighting the grey hair and wrinkles as fast as I can. Imagine bringing in a 22 year old girl that is an ex-prostitute and has daddy issues and she's desperate to get his attention.

One girl tried several times to get him alone for conversation in the other room. He laughed out loud and said "No, you can talk to me here in the kitchen."

I can imagine that if someone's marriage isn't secure enough (and I don't mean perfect because that doesn't exist) and if the husband is drawn in to be the shoulder for girls to cry on, then this ministry could end badly for them. I could totally see a girl become emotionally dependant on a man like that.

Know your strengths and weaknesses. Still, there may be battles sometimes with our girls about what they wear. We're not looking for burkas to be worn around here, but cover up the ta-tas before you come out of your room.

You'd think that wouldn't need to be told but I've had girls run from their room, to the bathroom, nude. I've had girls run around in their bra only. Sometimes I've thought it was intentional, and sometimes I've thought that they just aren't thinking this through.

My husband is a saint. He goes to the dump with regularity to throw away things like mattresses covered in period blood, bags of clothes left behind, old broken furniture, trash, donated items that are worthless, you name it. He cleans up after them and all of us.

The girls notice how he treats me and they think that he's an anomaly. They've never seen a man treat a woman that way. He cleans the kitchen, does the laundry, cares for our disabled son and loves his wife. He works hard as CEO of TWM keeping it running behind the scenes. He loves to see me work at my calling and supports me in it.

The girls love it. It gives them a role model to look for when they consider a relationship with someone, because they need to stop reaching for the lowest common denominator. They're worth more than that!

24
Carolyn

*Every morning as I ate breakfast with my brother and sister
before school, I knew what was next. I was supposed to go in
my mother and daddy's room and get in bed with him.*
-Carolyn Koontz Keys

At three years old, the night before her sister was born,
she remembers something terrifying happened. She
remembers it very clearly. Something extremely
traumatic happened that seared it into her memory.

It was one of the first times her own father molested her.

I can't imagine the confusion and fear that must have
created in her heart and mind. How does a three year old
girl even begin to process such a thing?

On the outside, her family seemed like the typical American family in the 1950's. Dad worked and made a good
living. Mom raised three kids in the early years, .two
girls and a boy. Carolyn was the oldest.

The extended family knew what was happening. In later
years, they spoke about it in hushed tones. They learned
lthat he had done it to other family members as well.

Her mother also had to have known. Her mother would
walk in the room at times and pretend not to see.

Nobody stepped in to stop it, so it continued until she was in her late teens and was able to summon the strength to put an end to it by saying no more! But this man didn't accept no for an answer. Even after she was married and had a child, he was still pursuing her, although now, unsuccessfully.

Then, the secret trauma was used against her by her abusive husband, in his fits of rage. His anger would always run to the one thing he knew would hurt her the worst.

He'd use this delicate information that was confided to him, as a tool of hatred against her. He would scream that nobody would ever want her because of what her father did to her. She was damaged goods, now. She was dirty, according to him.

I can only begin to imagine the pain and heartache on top of more pain and heartache. Shame on top of more shame.

It makes me very sad that while this was going on with my uncle, our family could have helped her at that time. We could have helped her escape a miserable situation.

Both of her parents are gone now. Her father died years ago and even now, all these years later, she still has nightmares that wake her in a pool of sweat. She's still afraid of this man as if he's still here and able to hurt her. These are scars that never go away.

This is my "Aunt Carolyn." She is brave and one of the kindest people I know. She's forgiving (to a fault) and thoughtful. I never met her father but the thought of him invokes an almost violent rage in me.

I know he must have been so very damaged himself to do such a thing, but we have got to protect children from these predators. How did this family all know and do nothing to help her? How does that happen?

I'm thankful that she has the courage to shed the light of day on her story. It makes people aware and may help another young girl, because of her story.

It's the first time we've ever had someone in their 70's live here before. Her situation is not the typical one we have had here at TWM. Instead, this is a place of rest that we are providing for her. This is a safe haven for Carolyn.

This is a home where she knows she's wanted and she knows she's secure because nothing is going to make her have to leave. She has found family in us, even though I'd seen her maybe twice in thirty years.

"Family" is often, not about blood.

She says she's never felt this kind of love before, with the exception of her son. She says she hasn't ever experienced this peace in her life before. She's never felt this wanted.

She's always felt like the black sheep in the family because of her father and what he did to her, and then subsequently, how they treated her because of it.

She brought a civil lawsuit against her father at one point when she was a young adult. Her entire family shunned her for years because of it. Even her mother. Eventually, she dropped the suit.

Carolyn still has nightmares about her father to this day, so many years later. She is still afraid. She has nightmares about her mother too. The mom she loved so much that never protected her from the monster that was her father.

Now she knows real love that is found and anchored in Jesus. That's what we're all about. Isn't that a reason to get up in the morning? To be able to make a huge difference in someone's life? If our little effort here, makes the rest of this wonderful woman's years, pleasant and happy, then who wouldn't do it?

If you have the opportunity to prove to someone through your own actions, that God loves them, then would you do it?

Carolyn, has always doubted that God could love her because she felt tainted, marred and dirty. Now she knows more and more with each passing day, that the Lord of all actually loves her and that she is so very valuable! What joy that brings to my heart!

25
When Someone Has to Leave

Just a small town girl,
livin' in a lonely world;
she took the midnight train goin' anywhere...
- Journey, "Don't Stop Believin"

I hate confrontation. I don't know anyone that doesn't. It's awkward. Just reminding someone to wash their hands as they reach for the refrigerator is awkward.

I'm constantly figuring out how to say things in the best possible way, so as not to be demeaning or embarrassing. But sometimes it just can't be helped.

When you have a girl that refuses to use basic hygiene and is just not teachable about it, it can get really difficult.

One girl here was using gauges in her earlobes. Each few days she's graduate up a step or two, so her earlobes were constantly crusty and she was constantly messing with them. She would remark about how they smelled like feta cheese.

So, I felt the need to literally follow her around at times making her wash her hands. I knew that if I didn't, she would have no thought of making food in the kitchen with those crusty fingers! I love her but not the crusty fingers!

There are many reasons for confrontation during a normal week here. Someone lashed out at another; Someone didn't come home on time; or someone used someone's shampoo. There were any number of issues to arise that required me intervening.

But the really tough ones were when I had to tell a girl she had to go.

Each time I've had to ask someone to move out, it was because they weren't making forward progress. I never made someone move out for sin or error.

People move forward or backward. There never seems to be a status quo. The girls I've asked to leave, have left because they actually went the opposite direction

One of them began staying out all night getting drunk. I told her that she cannot do that. She was ruining her life. Her drinking was escalating.

TWM is not a free hotel for someone to do whatever they want.

Another girl was really deteriorating day by day. She was stealing and breaking every rule more and more. Her attitude was so bad, she was mistreating everyone in the house, all the time. Yet, I still hated to have to do it. I felt so bad for her and felt even worse for her parents and grandparents who I also knew.

I sat with her out on the back porch and literally I was shaking. I had decided that if she responded well to what I was saying, then I would give her only a warning. But as I began going over the issues I had with her, she got defensive and angry. That was my answer.

I told her that she had to leave the next day. I get why someone in her situation would get defensive and angry. Maybe they always feel unwanted. Here is just another place that doesn't want them! This girl had been the "black sheep" of her family. She never felt like she fit in and this was one more place she didn't fit in.

I hate that. It makes me sad for her. Sometimes I'm in a hard corner though because I can't have volatile, violent behavior around the house. She was so volatile, our daughter, Alex slept on the floor in Theo's room that night.

This was really hard, for all of us. Remember, God really works through the toughest and roughest seas. He used this hard situation, to help this girl. She did go home the next day and she did well! She is now in college and holding down a good job.

We are far from perfect. I'm sure there are multiple ways in which I failed these girls. My hope is that they will see that I tried and hopefully I didn't damage them further. That is my greatest fear. Two girls left in handcuffs. One left in a manic state and left most of her belongings here, even her beloved guitar.

There was one girl years ago that left on her own accord. I would have asked her to leave had she not come up with the idea herself. That was easier for me! It wasn't a bad parting, but one that she thought was a good idea for her.

She had been here over two years and we were ready for her to move on, quite frankly. Don't judge us too harshly when I tell you that as she drove up the driveway, we asked the Amazon Alexa to play "Celebrate" by Kool & the Gang!

We may have even danced.

26
The Pool

Nothing brings out family disfunction like the holidays.
- Unknown

In the summer of 2018, I let the girls talk me into buying an above ground pool. I hate above ground pools. I've always thought they looked trashy. But I looked into it and saw that one with a pump and also rather large in size could be purchased for about three hundred bucks.

 I approached Marcus about it, and he immediately said "Absolutely not".

Well, I went to Wal-Mart and bought it anyway.

I couldn't lift it to bring it home.

Not only had I bought it unauthorized, I now had to call him to come and pick it up for me.

It's a wonder he sticks around.

He brought it home and laid it all the parts out on the carport. We all said we would help him put it together, but we all knew that it was mostly going to be him to do it. Needless to say, he was quite grumpy for two solid days about having to put this pool together.

And who could blame him?

When Pa does a project, he painstakingly does it to perfection. He is very precise and methodical. And we were pushing him to hurry it up and get it done! It was hot out! We couldn't wait to swim! Pa got grumpier and grumpier.

We picked the best possible place for it. Not quite level but I pushed some more, telling him it was level enough.

It wasn't.

About a hundred dollars of water later, it was spilling out one end and not even reaching the pump on the other end. We knew any swimming in this pool would end in the whole thing busting and we would go flying down the yard in a Funniest Home Video clip.

It had to be drained and redone. Marcus was fit to be tied and now, he was beyond grumpy. He was mad.

We let the pool drain into the yard and down to the creek overnight. By the next day, it was almost empty. So we all gathered around the pool and picked it up, moving it to another location so we could bring in fill dirt to level the original spot. Marcus had to get three loads of dirt in our truck to make the spot level. All of us with shovels! Pa was still mad.

We moved the pool back to it's original spot and proceeded to refill it.

The weight of the water made the fill dirt cave in some places so it was obvious right off the bat that it still wasn't going to be level. We decided we didn't care. It was more level than before and more importantly, the pump had water to it! We swam in it on July 4th, 2018. We had a cookout with hot dogs too.

Pa barely spoke to any of us (or at least that's how I remember it).

After five days, a lot of money, a lot of water, me learning pool chemicals, hard work and frustration, we had a pool to enjoy and we sure did. Only one neighbor could see it was crooked. A little embarrassing!

Of course, the cleaning of the pool landed on me with all my "free time." All the promises by the girls, of keeping it clean, fell by the wayside. I eventually got tired of cleaning it and the novelty wore off anyway. It had run its course.

We took it down 10 weeks later.

Well, Pa did. It's a wonder he stays.

27
Joy and Sam

Religion that is pure and undefiled before God the Father is this: to visit orphans and widows in their affliction, and to keep oneself unstained from the world.
- James 1:27

Marcus worked with this guy named Steve, years ago. Steve was clearly drinking on the job. It was getting worse and worse. Finally, Steve stopped coming to work.

A few weeks later, Marcus got a call from Steve. He needed some help. He needed money. He was crying and clearly distraught. So, we headed to Durham to meet Steve at Bojangles. We had some cash for him, about a hundred dollars, as I recall. Steve said his disabled son had died, his wife had been diagnosed with ovarian cancer and the family dog had also died.

We were broken hearted for this man. We didn't really even question the story of this huge man with tears streaming down his face, sipping on sweet tea at Bojangles. He only felt sorrow and pity for him.

A few weeks later, Marcus got a call from a lady named Joy. He was at work and couldn't chat with her long but she said she was Steve's wife and that Steve had suddenly died! Unable to stay on the phone, he gave her my number and said for her to call me.

I was standing in the middle of Kohl's when the call came. Her name was Joy and she wanted to tell us that Steve had died. She was calling because she remembered that Steve told her how Marcus had been kind to them, helping with the cash and that she was in desperate need.

She told me she and her disabled son were living in a motel with Steve when he passed. I was stunned when she said her disabled son was alive! I asked her to clarify.

Not only was Sam alive, but she did not have ovarian cancer and I clearly heard the family dog barking in the background! What in the world was going on? Who is dead and who is alive?

I drove to Durham after Marcus was able to confirm Joy's story about Steve's sudden demise. I met with Joy and Sam. Sam was in his late 20's with some form of Autism. I brought them fried chicken (Sam's favorite) and began to get to know their story. Steve had basically kept them in motels for years, like shut-ins.

They had no money and they owed over $700 to the motel for back rent. Steve had left them penniless and in debt. This older now single mama was in a desperate situation. Sam needed 24 hour care so she couldn't go to work. And without her, he would have to go to a group home or something like that. He'd just lost his dad, whom he dearly loved. He was distraught and clung to his stuffed animals, which all had names.

What would God have us do in this situation? It was clear to me and to our church. James 1:27 says, "Religion that is pure and undefiled before God, the Father, is this: to visit orphans and widows in their affliction, and to keep oneself unstained from the world."

We, and the good people at our church, helped to relocate them to Fuquay-Varina so that we can better minister to their needs and got them situated in an apartment. They were able to get set up on disability for Sam and Social Security for Joy. They were ok.

What if Marcus had never extended that kindness toward Steve? What if he had refused kindness because Steve was clearly spiraling. What if we had not noticed people in need or not been willing to take a step in aiding them in their despair? What would have happened to them? I cannot imagine.

Many people ask me where I find these folks in need. They're everywhere. Just be willing to see. Be open heart-ed to feel and be willing to get out of your comfort zone to love.

28
Racism is Not Tolerated

The refusal to act in the midst of injustice is itself an act of injustice. Indifference to oppression perpetuates oppression.
- Jemar Tisby, *The Color of Compromise*

A burning passion of mine is to help the African American community. They've endured so much in this country and as well in the American church throughout the years. I don't understand, for the life of me, how someone can love Jesus and still dislike (dare I say, even hate) a whole race of people, simply because of their skin color.

Y'all know Jesus wasn't white, right?

We that claim to love and follow Jesus must be about justice and these folks haven't had it since they were kidnapped and brought here. One look at the prison system will show you the truth of this.

If you're poor and black, you don't stand a chance. Does that matter to you? Does it bother you, my readers, that you can spend the rest of your life in prison, or be put to death, simply because you are black and can't afford an attorney that's decent? It bothers me. These are people made in God's image, just as much as you and I are.

I grew up hearing that God hasn't blessed their race. It's said as if God likes them less than whites. This is insanity.

The history of the African American people, if you choose to actually open your eyes and see it is that they have been oppressed for so long in this country, that they suffer under the weight of that. It's not that God likes them less; It's that they have been unjustly treated!

As a result of this oppression, I as a white female, want to do my part to make a difference. I want to do what little I can to reverse the effects of what my people have done. It's my form of reparations.

Racism is still alive and well and if you don't believe that, then you don't want to see it.

Just last week, one of my girls, who is black, went to the eye doctor and was humiliated by the white receptionist, because she was poor and black.

It was everything I could do to stop myself from going over there and giving that lady a piece of my mind. Nothing seems to make me more angry than one person talking down to another because of their skin tone.

How absurd is that?

What's even worse is racism within the church. People of God making jokes, making statements about a race of people that are demeaning and degrading should never ever happen. It offends God. It should offend us all.

I urge you to read *The Color Of Compromise* by Jemar Tisby. It chronicles how racism has been alive and well throughout the history of the American church and in particular, the Presbyterian church, which is my denomination. It's shocking and disturbing and a must read.

Y'all know Jesus wasn't white, right?

29
Rules and Regulations

Unheard-of combinations of circumstances
demand unheard-of rules.
- Charlotte Brontë, *Jane Eyre*

Our rules were listed in Chapter 7. Now I'll cover the rationale behind them, and how they have evolved.

1. Church on Sunday with the family is so important because it helps solidify the feeling of family, which is belonging somewhere. Also, faith in God is vital in someone overcoming addictions and problems.

2. No taking the Lord's name in vain became a thing for me because I cannot stand "God Dammit" or "Jesus" being used as a curse word. I tell them they can use "Buddha Dammit" if they must use something.

3. We discourage sexual relations because they're here at TWM to work on themselves, not to date and repeat mistakes.

4. No getting wasted because it's wrong and you end up doing stupid stuff. One of my girls would go out and over drink and disappear for days.

5. No illegal drugs. I have found marijuana and caught a few smoking it as well here. I've found infused gummy bears and some half-cut straws, used for snorting.

6. Pornography. Our pornography rule is for a multitude of reasons and it's often a rule that's not kept! But we know addiction takes some time to overcome:

a. I believe pornography is a direct assault on women. The exact women we're trying to help in fact.

b. Women who are addicted to drugs or trafficked are largely the ones participating in this. Let's not be a part of continuing that.

c. Some pornography is illegal.

d. It is an affront to God, who made us in His image.

7. No dating. A common theme with young adults in this culture is dating sites used for casual sex hook-ups.

Not only is there a no dating rule, but along with that, there is a no dating site account rule. No Plenty of Fish, No Whisper, No Tinder accounts.

8. Jobs. Everyone works.

9. Everyone saves and/or pays off fines, charges, tickets, court costs etc. I had one girl come home with a new pair of one hundred dollar boots once.

I don't even spend one hundred dollars on boots!

Financial accountability is important. Sometimes I watch bank statements. Sometimes I confiscate debit cards. Whatever is needed to learn to save. One of my girls was spending four hundred dollars per month on fast food, when I provide thousands of dollars of good food here for them for free. There was an addiction there.

10. Hygiene is a persistent problem. One we found out by trial and error. Most of these girls don't even know about basic hygiene. Sometimes they've never been taught to brush their teeth, for example.

11. Washing hands when you enter the kitchen!! I will often put signs up everywhere when someone new moves in. It's a habit that must be learned. It's very uncomfortable to have to remind someone of this when they open the refrigerator."Have you washed your hands?" They'll often say "Yes, in the bathroom!" But if I don't see it happen or hear it happen, it didn't happen.

12. 10:00 curfew so I can lock the door at night and go to sleep. Sometimes rules like this need to be bent at times.

13. Room and bed made daily. Again, these basics are often not taught to them so we're making new habits.

14. Extending kindness and grace is vital to this many people living in one house. In the same way, I tell the girls that I will also let them down at times and I hope they'll extend me the same grace.

15. One daily chore is required. It's like pulling teeth sometimes to get them to do a five-minute daily chore. But it's all about learning new habits.

These rules are *all* broken from time to time. It's not a three strikes and you're out kind of thing. We try to show grace.

I want to see growth. Change. Even baby steps. We've even had girls fake illness to get out of going to church. Then the kitchen camera catches them milling about just fine. We have watched them while sitting in church a time or two!

30
Vacations

I need a vacation, from my vacation
- Ma

Each year, TWM has been given a beach trip for a week on Topsail Island. One of our board members, Laura Jacimore, has rented a huge house and our biological kids and some of our grandkids go as well as the our dear friends, the Hunt family.

It's always fancy and right on the water with a pool.

Throughout the years, I've vacillated about who gets to go with us. Do we take whichever girls that live here at the time? Do we take past girls that have gotten to go before? Or do we go without them and give me a break from everything?

I work so hard to make these girls feel like they're part of the family and then am I supposed to turn around and say they're not actually family, so they aren't invited. It's always a huge problem for me because people put pressure on me to not bring them.

I don't see them as "bringing my work" with me on vacation. I'm actually so excited to show them such a lovely time in a dream of a house on the beach. They've never experienced anything like it before! That's a thrill for me.

121

One year, I didn't take them. It was a mistake.

It was a free-for-all! There was drama from the house from the beginning. They got to do all the things Ma wouldn't have allowed, including sneaking a guy in for the night. This guy was the sperm donor for her son. An Xbox thug, who lives with mommy.

A drug dealer. In my house. He wasn't even supposed to know our address, much less be in my house.

That was the only year we haven't taken them to the beach.

Each year, the question arises again. Who is going? It's almost like mental torment for me. Is this girl going to be moved out before we go and if so, she can or can't go?

Who and how many will be living here when September comes? How many rooms do we need? Which of my bio-logical kids are coming and do they resent me bringing TWM girls? Who's paying for and cooking all the food all week?

If one girl has a baby, does she get a whole room to her-self? If not, who wants to stay in a room on vacation with a baby that cries at night? Who will room with who? Who's complaining about having to room with someone? Who's going to make sure this girl or that girl stays close to the house and doesn't wander off at night?

122

Who's going to pay for everyone if we want to go out for seafood one day? Do I have time to plan ahead to save money and buy the groceries in advance for 15 people and then lug it all down there in multiple coolers?

Part of me says forget it. No more vacations! Vacations are exhausting.

One year, I rented a house in the mountains in the fall. We were making special memories with our friend, Preston Hunt who was diagnosed with brain cancer. We had such fun. We had a crawfish boil, played Cajun music and danced.

On Sunday morning, we had a little church service and Marcus served us communion. Those are some sweet memories. Our friend died in January of 2018 and so, I'm especially thankful that we were able to make those memories with him and his family.

I like to think that the girls who have been able to vacation with us have really enjoyed it, and have sweet memories as a result. Many of my girls have never flown on a plane! I dream of taking them on a plane to New York City to see a play, but I've never been able to afford that.

I can picture their faces as they see Times Square in person. I would love to show them Phantom Of The Opera on Broadway! My girls have never even had something so lovely in their life. How fun would that be to see them experience some of what many take for granted?

31
Underwear on the Floor

Holly, please get the clothes out of the dryer.
I don't know whose they are and I'm not touching them.
- Pa

My poor husband. He's this manly man kind of guy and he lives with all these women!

He works tirelessly cleaning up the house, doing laundry and keeping the kitchen clean. He does my laundry, his and Theo's.

Time and time again, the girls would forget to move their laundry from the washer to the dryer, or from the dryer to their baskets, or take their baskets to their rooms. When we only had one washer and dryer, this was especially frustrating for Marcus.

He did not want to ever touch the girls clothes because they had bras and underwear in there! So, he would text the house with "Whoever has clothes in the dryer, please remove them."

They'd say "Sorry Pa" and then it would happen again the next day with someone else.

One time, Pa had to reboot the modem which was in one of the girl's room. That was the time he discovered underwear on the modem to hide the lights.

We had one girl here for many months and she had a habit of dropping articles of clothing everywhere she went. So, I would get a text from Marcus, "Someone's underwear is on the floor in the laundry room."

He would be so mad about it! It always made me laugh! I'd text the girls to find out whose it was and tell them to go get them.

It was really bad when somehow one of the girl's article of clothing ended up in our laundry basket so he washed and dried them along with our clothes. I'd say, "These undies aren't mine." He would just almost die!

We had to make a rule for the girls to put their dirty towels in the main laundry basket otherwise they would pile up in their rooms and we would run out of clean towels. So, then Marcus was washing towels all the time.

Finally we got a second washer and dryer donated to us by a friend of TWM.

This was freedom for Marcus because now the girls had their own set and he had one for the three of us. He no longer had the problem of someone's clothes sitting in there.

When you live with people, you're in close quarters for months and sometimes years! So, there are nearly constant adjustments to be made to make it work.

32
Mom

Ah, but nobody said life was fair, Tina.
I'm bigger and I'm faster. I will always beat you.
- Joan Crawford, *Mommy Dearest*

Her story was the most shocking I'd ever heard. I'm retelling it now because I want to help people understand that so many of my girls have come from horrific life situations. When you hear something like this, you can't help but weep and have mercy.

Throughout her life, she was taken to big Wake Hospital in Raleigh many times growing up for various broken bones and other injuries like burns to her face and body.

Her mother was her tormentor. Every day of her life. Every day. Raging, uncontrolled fury was unleashed on her from as far back as she could remember. She doesn't remember a time as a child when she wasn't afraid.

Imagine your life at five, six years old. What was it like?

Her mother would often have to keep her home from school because of the injuries she'd inflicted on her baby girl. She would tell her that if she told anyone, she would kill her. Did the doctors and nurses at the hospital ever happen to see the blank stare in the little girl's eyes that were reaching out for help?

On the worst days, the torture took on a sexual nature. Her mother would tie her hands and feet to the bedposts, sit on her tummy and beat her crotch area with a belt.

This girl, now in her 30's, is kind and sweet, with a huge beautiful smile. She loves Jesus, and she's a mess. We met in Zaxbys for lunch and I bawled like a baby hearing her story. She has lost all six of her own children to foster care because she's addicted to cocaine. She calls it her "powders."

My heart cannot take the sadness I feel for this girl. And can I say right here, that I would be using "powders" too if I had her life. So, we have a choice here. Judge her for her "powder" use, or have compassion and mercy.

This is a "worst case scenario" so to speak. But I've seen so much damage on girls from parents and particularly, mothers. I've seen girls that have so many roadblocks in their lives, because mom didn't give them affection. If you don't feel bonded with your child, then fake it till you feel it.

Kids need to feel loved and secure. Kids need the loving touches of their mother. If you feel like you're holding back for some reason, get some help and again, fake it till you feel it. Your child's entire future could depend on it.

New moms, you have this tiny human born to you, and that girl or boy has a complex emotional makeup that has to have nurturing.

Don't hold back. Hugs and kisses all the time. Say 'yes"
as much as possible and lay down your life for them. You
have to put their needs first. Who else will?

I've said it before, the girls we serve have often felt like
the black sheep of their family. What does that tell me?

It tells me that they didn't get the nurturing and affection and acceptance that the rest of them got or that they
needed. That can send them down this road to self de-
struction and addiction, because they feel worthless.

I was nineteen when my first child was born. I had no
idea how to be totally free in my affection for her. I held
back. I was afraid of her actually. Is that connected to her
present addictions? Could be. Learn from my mistakes.

If you're a Christian, new, or soon-to-be new mother,
then please know right up front that your kids are going
to screw up. A lot. I know you think you know how to
parent and everyone else is open game for your criticism.
Your kids would never do this or that. They will.

Pray for them, and when they mess up, find ways to
inspire their obedience. Don't ever make them feel that
they are loved less because they mess up. Everyone mess-
es up. Tell them when you mess up. Ask them to forgive
you. If you're not doing that regularly, you need to start.

These is the front lines in the drug war: motherhood.

If you're an older mom like me and you reflect on mistakes you made with your kids, then go to them now. Tell them you're sorry. Be specific. Hugs and kisses still needed.

33
Island of Misfit Toys
You'll never fit in!
- Boss Elf, "Rudolph The Red Nosed Reindeer"

Sundays have been the most challenging for us but also the most refreshing. I learned from my mom how to put out a Sunday spread.

Most Sundays, we've had huge crowds here for a feast. The friendship and the love of one another, with what I like to say is a bunch of misfits, including me. We've often remarked about how TWM is that island of misfit toys from *Rudolph The Red Nosed Reindeer.*

As I've said previously, the girls have felt like black sheep in their families. They feel like they don't fit in. It's important to me to make them feel like they "fit" in here, because ultimately, that's what's missing in their lives.

We all want to be a part of something, to be an integral part of something and accepted for who we are.

In TWM kitchen, there's this huge pine table with long benches for seating. I can fit 12 around that easily. Then there are other places to sit and eat as well, like the dining room and in the living room, especially during football season! We have roaring fires in the fireplace and when there's no football, there's always music.

We have an Amazon Alexa in the kitchen and the girls are often screaming at her to play this or that song! We dance and sing to rock and roll. We dance, sing and raise hands to praise music and we laugh a lot.

When I'm in my room and I hear the girls laughing and becoming actual sisters, it makes me tear up because these relationships are precious. Our daughter, Alex will be the maid of honor in one of our past resident's wedding coming up.

These are bonds that will last forever. It's family. We laugh like family. We argue like family and even fight sometimes, but we love each other, so we forgive.

Many girls that haven't lived here, I've worked to serve them in other ways. They are often here at the house on Sundays, along with some guys that we've ministered to over the years.

34
Pa's Laundry Rules

Etiquette, Customs and Mores for Laundry

We have received generous donations in money and appliances for TWM so we can more efficiently launder our clothes. There are two washers and two dryers, now!

One washer/dryer set will be for Ma and Pa, and the other set will be for the girls. Be grateful, considerate and responsible for these donated appliances.

1. Wash more frequently, rather than big loads.

2. Do not leave the house with clothes in the washer/dryer.

3. Do not move someone else's clothes from the washer to the dryer, or from the dryer.

4. Stay on top of the progress of your clothes.

5. Do not take your clothes to the laundry and set them down.

6. Do not take your clothes out of the dryer and set them down.

7. Do not wash or dry clothes late at night.

8. Clean your basket with a cleaner before putting clean clothes in it.

9. Do not attempt to renegotiate these rules.

10. Be considerate of the gifts you have been given. Plan for the future.

35
The Seminary Years

If I speak in the tongues of men or of angels, but do not have
love, I am only a resounding gong or a clanging cymbal.
- 1 Corinthians 13:1

In 1990, our family landed in Jackson, Mississippi for
four years of seminary training for Marcus. Those were
financially very hard years but also we made some dear
friends there that we've cherished until this day. So, there
are a lot of good memories, and some bad ones.

The years in seminary taught us both a lot of life lessons
and I'm sure Marcus learned a lot of theology while there
but seminary in no way prepared us for actual ministry.

What I garnered from that time is that we would be the
elite in churches where we would serve and we should
have our personal relationships outside of where we
served. We can't let our guards down with our own congregants. If you carry that on to its end, it means we treat
congregants as projects, not human beings. That is false
and damaging teaching.

Never at seminary did we learn what ministry is like in
the real world. Learning the finer points of the Hebrew
language would prove most helpful when you're trying
to love a prostitute. Or telling a drug addict that Post-
Millennialism is the right view of the end times. I think
they would just wish for the end of times at that point.

Theology is not unimportant. I'm not arguing that. What I am arguing is that people who love Jesus and have a desire to serve in ministry have got to be equipped and prepared better.

I don't care how brilliant a seminary student is or how gifted he is in the pulpit, if he doesn't have compassion then he (or she) is like a clanging cymbal (I Cor. 13:1). A clanging cymbal is loud, obnoxious and drives people away.

Seminaries need to send people out to do actual ministry work before they graduate them. The students need to work in the inner city getting to see what lies ahead if they want to actually help people. Or, they need to do counseling in a pregnancy center. They need to be showing hospitality to their neighbor, no matter what they believe or look like.

During our seminary years, I did prison ministry work at the women's state prison in Jackson. That was my very first foray into what the world looks like outside of my white, middle class, evangelical, Christian world.

It was shocking to me, I'm not gonna lie. It smelled bad and it looked gross. I didn't want to touch anything or anybody. The truth of the matter was, those women were more kind to me, than I was to them.

We held services in the chapel. I was in charge of it once a month, so I brought in "reformed" preachers.

All men, of course because God forbid a woman teach! Literally shaking my head. I was going to "fix" this lesbian problem with some of these women, with the word of God! Shaking my head again.

I was taken to meet one African American lady in solitary that was dying of ovarian cancer. Her cell was hot (Mississippi in the summer with no air condition!) and humid, reeking of old blood and body odor.

When we entered, her smile was huge and beautiful. At least that's how I see it in my memory. At the time, I saw nothing beautiful. The lady chaplain with me knelt down on the floor in front of this poor, dying lady and gently touched her. She gave this dying human a loving touch and kind words while I stood there looking on with horror.

God, please forgive me for not loving on her! It was all I could do to keep from throwing up. This dying woman was a sister in Christ. She loved her Jesus. She is with him and I will see her again! But my heart was a clanging cymbal. I wasn't ready to minister to anyone! It would take many more years before my eyes became open and my heart became soft to the hurts and cares of people, especially people different than me.

36
Date Night

Date night; it's cheaper than marriage counseling.
- Jerry Seinfeld

Marcus and I have to make sure we get time together. To accomplish that, we have "Date Night" where we go in our room with something yummy to eat from a restaurant, some wine and a movie to watch.

This is the sign Marcus made and taped to our door whenever we had a date night.

Date Night

Knock not -- live

Knock -- die

Text -- die tomorrow

My plan for our room is to have our little corner of the house. Nobody is allowed to come in there.

That almost never works. They gravitate to it! I do have a beautiful bed with expensive linen sheets. It's our haven of rest, our place to retreat.

37
One Baby Daddy, Two Baby Mommas

B-A-B-Y-M-A-M-A
This goes out to all my baby mamas
This goes out to all my baby mamas
B-A-B-Y-M-A-M-A
This goes out to all my baby mamas
I got love for all my baby mamas
- Fantasia Barrino

Years ago, before we decided to serve women exclusively, we had a young man around twenty-one years old, named Jemal live here for a time. He had so many road-blocks to overcome.

We wanted to help. I genuinely loved him, and still do! He's one of my favorite kids we've worked with. He has a simple faith and he is very kind. He lived here for a few months and became one of my kids. He even calls me mom. However, his time here wasn't that long because of the same issue so many of my kids struggle with and that is addiction. He wasn't ready to work on it. He had to go.

He left on good terms with me but I went to bed that day and cried for the next two or three days (I cry a lot). My heart was so sad. Many times I feel as though I don't help anyone at all. I feel like a failure and that day, I felt like quitting altogether. I voiced this to a few people that got me back on track but I really felt defeated.

138

A few years later, we had Leslie living here with her son, Adam. Adam was one year old. We didn't even have any open rooms available at that time, so we hung curtains in the basement from the ceiling and made a room of sorts for them. It's in the basement dungeon but at least they had some privacy and it was better than a homeless shelter.

Leslie was a really sweet girl and she loved her son very much. She wanted the best for him but that was made complicated because she had some mental challenges that I wasn't previously aware of. Almost all the girls that come here have at the very least, high anxiety. They have it for good reason.

Their lives have been rough. They've endured more than I have ever even thought about. I've seen many girls get triggered by something that you'd never think was a trigger, but whatever it was, it would take them back to trauma that occurred in their lives.

Leslie was no exception. So, her coping mechanisms were not the best. Mostly, she would sneak away to smoke pot. It relaxed her brain. If it were legal, I'd be all for it for someone like her.

She also had a hard time with basic tasks. But we had hours and hours of conversation in the evenings out back on the porch. She would play her guitar and we would sing. I think it was the first time she had ever felt loved by a family.

Soon Jan moved in as well. She was pregnant. These girls knew each other already. In another chapter, I talk about how this was a mistake. They often got the best of me.

The father of Jan's unborn baby, was the same baby daddy of Leslie's child, Adam. Let that sink in a moment. Two girls at TWM and both of them were made pregnant by the same guy. and that guy was our "son" Jemal that had lived a few years before!

You'd think that this arrangement wouldn't go well; two women with babies from the same father. Yet the two girls got along very well! Too well, in fact. Unbeknownst to me, they were also sleeping together down in the basement. You know, the kind of sleeping where you are not sleeping!

You can't make this stuff up. I didn't realize this until they were packing their stuff up to move out, together.

They got a kick out of how they'd snowed me really well. It still makes me laugh to think back on it. The whole situation was bizarre and to this day, it's one of my favorite stories to tell.

38
Bible Studies

All Scripture is breathed out by God and profitable for teaching
for reproof, for correction, and for training in righteousness.
- 2 Timothy 3:16

I used to have this image in my mind, of what it would look like for me to teach Bible studies (or book studies) to the girls that lived here. I had this lovely picture conjured up in my mind about smiling women gathered around the hearth with Ma, listening to her "wealth of wisdom" on various subjects and the girls following every word.

It's never looked like that.

The reality is, countless times, I've sat down with three or four of them at a time, on various occasions, to begin reading together. One time, I began reading aloud the first chapter of a book and couldn't get through the second paragraph without beginning to cry.

I looked up and they're all in tears as well. The book was on shame. We made it through that chapter after a while because everyone wanted to share and give opinions.

The next week, we tried for the second chapter and because of work schedules, we were less one person. We decided to wait for them. The next week, a different girl wasn't home. We gave up after that.

For a while we tried to have Bible reading at suppertime, but we ended up only being together for a meal at the table on Sundays.

I attempted to have one-on-one time with a few of the girls, reading and praying together. That also fizzled out after a few times.

In a house like this one, there are several adults (and sometimes a child or two) and everyone has different schedules, going in different directions, so it's difficult to plan to do anything all together, except for Sundays.

Then you have the problem of watching a show without someone, or reading all together without one person present. You can imagine the hurt feelings. Then I get the "just chuck it" idea in my head, because that's just how I am. Forget it. Never trying that again.

As a last resort, I began writing Bible verses on the dry erase board. I even encouraged them to memorize some of them. That was a fun exercise that everyone seemed to enjoy and get into. So, that's the extent of my lovely bible reading, of late.

Often, we've gotten offers from people to come "teach" my girls the bible. No kidding. Well intentioned people call (some we know and some we don't) and say they want to volunteer with us. We get all excited and then they let us know that they only want to teach the girls.

The first time this happened I was like, "You want to what?" So, here's my disclaimer about giving people access to TWM girls. Not gonna happen.

At the very least, it would have to be:
a. Someone we know well;
b. someone the girls know, like and are comfortable with;.
c. someone with whom I have great respect;
d. someone that is also willing to clean the bathroom;
e. someone that I know would not shame the girls with anything they say.

I get it though. I get how the thought could occur. So, they are more than welcome to go start a non-profit of their own and teach the residents there.

It's highly unlikely that my ladies will be subjected to anyone other than me or Pa, even if we're stumbling around through it.

39
The Flipper

The worst option is the flipper, also known as
an acrylic removable partial denture.
- Dental Economics

In 2005, I was in a family water balloon fight that somehow ended in a glass of water that accidentally hit my
face. The event caused me to need two front tooth root
canals.

Fast forward to 2015 and I noticed that the most front
tooth was turning brown. I ended up with a broken root
when the dentist attempted to clean out the previous root
canal. That meant the tooth had to come out.

This was devastating to me as you can imagine! A little
research showed that a tooth implant could cost thousands of dollars. Actually, the first dental specialist was
going to charge me around ten grand for the whole
process which I did not have. So, I had the tooth removed
and a flipper was made for me to wear to cover the enormous, awful gap right in front of my face. This contrap-
tion seemed to envelop my whole mouth!

It was more like a retainer. It was so uncomfortable and
I hated it. I couldn't even eat with it in. If I was having
lunch with someone, or had Sunday lunch company (as
we did almost every Sunday!), I'd go to great lengths to
take it out when the other person wasn't looking!

Then take a bite of food and slip it back in my mouth asap!

I was able to do this discreetly and I don't think people ever knew. Imagine having to spit that huge thing out of your mouth with slobber and remnants of lunch all over it then cupping it in in your hand while chewing (and covering your mouth with the other hand, by the way, because they would see the indentation where there is no tooth! This was a well choreographed dance mind you.

You have to time it just right. Spit out tooth with the left hand. Use fork to place food in mouth with right hand. Put fork down quickly. Cover mouth while chewing. Then reverse the process when the guest looked away to get it back in your mouth to speak.

And I couldn't just take it out and eat while having conversation because; well, because!

I looked like someone that had been using drugs for years!

During the day at home, I kept it out. It was just too uncomfortable to wear. One time I forgot that it wasn't in my mouth when a delivery guy rang the doorbell. I answered the door with my usual big toothless smile! So, after that, I decided that I needed to have it on my person somewhere in case of unexpected visitors. So, I kept it in my bra!

This was about the time that Beth moved in. She had been homeless for a few years and her only friends were homeless addicts, who had lost teeth! So, she loved this about me! She said I made her feel at home.

For a year and a half, I lived with this huge front tooth gap and a flipper in my bra. Honestly, if I had ten grand to spend on an implant, I don't think I could have justified it in my mind for something cosmetic, when I see so many people that have nothing to their name.

During that year and a half, it became a Welcome Mission family joke! Everyone loved that I was toothless. The flipper got stretched out enough that I could flip it in and out with a simple movement of my tongue. It became a constant movement that I did without even thinking. It gave me a little relief from the uncomfortableness of it when it was only partially in. And it freaked little kids out!

A friend told me about an advertisement on the radio for dental implants. The price was two grand! I went for it! Within three months, I had my implant. I was whole again. I could eat now without concern. I could stop the flipper dance at meals! I was free!

That Christmas, the girls all insisted that the flipper had to be in place of the star on the top of our Christmas tree. There it was for all to see. Superglued to the very top. My flipper.

40
I Just Want to Help

Quitting smoking is easy. I've done it hundreds of times.
- Mark Twain

Several years ago, I drove down south of Dunn, NC in my white mini-van to see a girl I'd met a few times before, that needed help in a variety of ways. She had texted me and asked me to come see her.

That trip took me an hour each way. That's not necessarily a bad thing, depending. But over time, I've seen that if someone wants something badly enough, they will get where they need to be, or want to be. They're very industrious when they want to be somewhere.

It dawned on me that I was chasing these girls down to help them. There was no need for me to drive 120 miles that day to see this girl, when she could have come to me for the help she needed. Once that realization came to me, it changed so much about how I do things and saved me a lot of time that could be spent on another girl.

I will often get a call or text from someone saying, "Hey would you call so-in-so because she needs help." I reply that no, I won't call them but give them my number, I'd be happy to talk to them and help where I'm able. That has a two-fold reasoning behind it. One, I'm not doing the chasing and two, it shows me if the girl has any initiative to help herself.

147

I can't walk for someone but I can walk with them. So, right off the bat, I have some indication if the girl wants a hand-up or a hand-out. I've done my share of hand outs, like with food, but if someone wants real help from us, I need to see that they're willing to walk with us.

I will see some of the same patterns in most of these girls. They get in a fight with their mom or boyfriend and contact me immediately, needing a place to stay.

I listen to their concerns and tell them to call me tomorrow or the next day and we'll see what we can do. Every single time that's happened, the girl never calls me back, until the next explosive event. This is one way that I can tell that they're not ready for real change yet.

But I'll be here waiting and willing when they're ready

41
Pornography

*Surveys say that one in three women watch porn
at least once a week*
- Fight The New Drug

There are a lot of common problems that our girls often struggle with. My job is to help them, encourage them, and remind them of God's love for them.

Pornography is an addiction that is very hard to overcome. I've had girls here that have really battled it. I think people often think that it's a man's issue but I think it is quite common in women as well, especially in women that have suffered from sexual abuse.

I want this book to show the real life hardships that exist here at TWM. I don't want to be too graphic in some of these because it can bring added shame to an already piled up shame that they often face each day.

With my background, having never had this struggle, it's been a journey for me to understand it and know how to deal with it in a way that helps our girls overcome it. God loves us where we are, but we're not to stay there! We need to be putting off the "old man/woman" and moving toward a more Christ-like person every day. Because of my background, I've honestly had the "ick" factor in my heart toward these types of things. I'll be honest, it grosses me out.

My challenge has been to handle these moments with the grace of God while encouraging turning away from sin, without showing any "grossed out" or "ick" attitude.

If one of my girls loves Jesus with her whole heart, but because of her past as a child, is tempted and sometimes fails in this battle, my job is to remind her to take it to the cross and LAY IT DOWN. Jesus bore that FOR her. He loves her THAT much.

He forgives as far as the east is from the west. Lay it down there, with the shame and the lies of the devil that she is no good or at the worst, not loveable. If I can show her that I still love her knowing what I know, then she begins to see that maybe Jesus can too.

I also want so badly to be approachable. If I shamed them when they admitted their struggles to me, that would shut them down from coming to me for help.

We've done the "Covenant Eyes" apps and other apps that are supposed to deter the use of porn, but let's face it, where there's a will, there's a way and this generation will ALWAYS be able to outmaneuver this old girl with electronics.

I'm not doing that any more. Sometimes I guess it can be a helpful tool, but my experience here, is that the best avenue to take is through the heart.

My direction is to keep pressing the truths of Jesus to the heart and showing them that his ways bring life. Maybe removing some temptation by requesting that all phones be left in the kitchen at night is prudent, but to tell you the truth, sometimes pornography is way down the list of things I need address to begin with.

42
Mistakes I've Made

The steadfast love of the Lord never ceases;
His mercies never come to an end.
- Lamentations 3:22

The only way to do a ministry like this is to either learn from someone that's done it or do it by trial and error. I did it through the latter. I didn't have anyone to talk to and ask questions about what to do in this or that situation. I had no one to tell me that a decision I was about to make would be the wrong one because this is what would happen.

I have my husband and my board, but none of us have seen a ministry like this one. So, I've made many mistakes. Too many to count, but I'll highlight some of them here for anyone that is contemplating a ministry like this.

I can honestly say that the biggest mistake I've made is time and time again letting people outside the loop of TWM sway my own opinions and decisions. I can recount so many times when I would give too much weight to the opinions of others.

I think that stems from worrying too much about how others think of me. I hate this about myself but I give way too much care for how I'm seen and viewed, although I have grown in this area a lot over the last few years.

I learned the hard way to not let girls that live here, date. Now, if you move in, you're single. Period. Dating only distracts from their focus on themselves and their goals. They can date later.

I've made mistakes early on with believing lies. I'm much more savvy now. No, you don't have tooth pain for the seventh time in a year. No, you're not eating an apple in the front yard at midnight, with smoke coming out of it and a bad stench.

No, you're not sick, you're going to church. No, you didn't spend that much at the grocery store. I know you got cash to hide it from me for fast food.

No, you aren't just sleepy with those squinty eyes and smirk on your face. No, you weren't given a brand new expensive purse with the tags still on it from a customer through the drive thru window. No, you didn't do your chore, because I just did it and it was filthy. No, you didn't wash your hands before exiting the bathroom. I listened.

Another obvious mistake I made early on was letting two friends live here. Girls who had been friends before coming here. They outnumbered me. I felt at a disadvantage from day one. They could cover for one another. Alibis for each other. Sneak off to smoke pot and gang up on me with a plausible story. They'd talk behind our backs and scheme. It was miserable. I'll never do that again.

153

I have to have the upper hand so to speak. Otherwise, I feel like there are enemies living under our roof. Do you have any idea how it feels to have someone that you think is an outright enemy living with you? This could be someone that could hurt you, given the chance.

Many times we've taken extra precautions to protect Theo and the rest of us, like several more surveillance cameras (including one in Theo's room that feeds into our room). I think it's a good thing that I'm naturally suspicious now. It's taken time to learn.

One time those two girls were down on the back porch with a couple of friends that they asked to visit. I knew something was amiss. I could feel it.

We listened in and watched from the camera that's right over that table. We had to do that many times over the years. It's in plain view, but the girls forget it's there. That was stupid of me to even allow those particular friends to come over.

I've also learned that these girls we serve cannot manage money. Ever. They need help. They need accountability.

Now, nothing surprises me.

Checking account transparency is absolutely necessary. All of a sudden they have money because they're working and getting paychecks!

One girl worked for months and saved over 700 bucks. She moved out and spent it all in a weekend. That was supposed to go toward a car. Now, I want to see the account statement when it comes and I might want to keep their debit card in the safe. Another girl was using her debit card to pay for everyone's lunches at work.

She had no idea how much of her money was gone. I want them to be generous. Let's figure out how much per month they can give. Tithe. Budget it. Then save.

Not everyone is going to be behind our work here. People in my own family don't support us. That was a huge and hard realization for me. I'm not necessarily talking about monetary support either. I'm saying that some won't even ask me how we're doing or how are girls are.

I can't decide if they don't care of if they disagree with me doing this. I have no idea. It's like this weird elephant in the room and nobody mentions it's there.

I've been accused of running this ministry for ulterior motives. I don't get paid a single dime. I have Christian friends and family that look at me suspiciously. I don't get it. It makes me cry when I think about it, so I don't.

God has called us to this. He has. And as each year passes I care less and less about what people think or who supports us and who doesn't. It's his work. It's his ministry. I will not stop unless he closes the doors.

43
King Theo

Theo is the best person ever.
- Everyone

When I was 35, I found out I was pregnant with our only son. We were over the moon happy after having five girls in a row. Our second baby girl, named Lindsey died shortly after birth in 1985 and I had to be given a blood transfusion due to complications with her birth.

Blood transfusions at that time were more than a little risky. They had just six months earlier developed a test to determine if AIDS was in blood. The transfusion I received was AIDS free. Unbeknownst to me, I did get a Hepatitis antibody from that transfusion. Because of that antibody, the pregnancy with our son got complicated.

Doctors had to do several amniocentesis during the pregnancy to monitor the state of his blood. One day my specialist said, "We'll do a genetic study this time, since we're taking amniotic fluid anyway." That seemed reasonable to me although in our minds, abortion wasn't an option if there was a problem with the baby.

We thought it might be good to know in advance if there were issues. I remember being very nonchalant about it. Not a care in the world. I was finally having my boy.

We went in to the doctor's office a few weeks later. We'd planned to swing over to Home Depot afterward because we were forever working on our house. But the doctor's words stopped us in our tracks. All I remember is hearing Down Syndrome and that every cell they looked at was affected.

We walked out of there like zombies. The tears came in the car. "I don't want a baby with Down Syndrome!" I screamed to Marcus and especially to God. Why has God done this to me? I was distraught, to put it mildly.

Sometimes, our hard providences end up being our best blessings.

Theophilus Paul Rench was born December 11th, 2000. I was so afraid. I thought the nurses would hide him in the back of the nursery so onlookers wouldn't be able to see him.

Nothing could be farther from the truth.

In fact, the nurses fought over him! He didn't cry, and he was by FAR the cutest baby in that hospital.

As of writing this book, our precious and favorite child Theo, is eighteen years old.

Some of his favorite things to do at TWM include slamming doors to startle people, then die laughing running down the hall.

He loves to get reactions from people. I have to tell people to remember to lock their doors when in the bathroom or in their room getting dressed because Theo will open the doors to make sure who's in there! When the girls are out back on the porch, he sits up in his second floor window and waves at them, speaking to them in a language we don't understand, and of course, laughing.

Theo sits at one spot at the kitchen table and in one certain chair in the living room. Those are his. King Theo will literally make you move if you're in his seat.

He takes his Nerf sword everywhere he goes. He steals cloth napkins from restaurants by slipping them into his pocket. He has been known to take menus as well, but those are harder to hide on the way out the door. Theo loves to collect church bulletins. He has hundreds. His favorite food is Chick-fil-A. We finally disposed of hundreds of kids meals toys when we gave away his dresser.

Theo is the joy of TWM. Everyone loves "brother" and he delights in all the attention. I've often thought about how good TWM is for him. Otherwise, his life would be quite boring. There's so much life here! Activities all the time! He gets more love from this extended family and he gives love when someone is low and needs a hug.

When God gave us this baby with an extra chromosome, I fought against it immediately! It went against my plans and my vision for my family. And now look. He's the greatest asset of this ministry and this family.

44
Reality Check

You are stronger than you believe.
You have greater powers than you know.
- Antiope to Diana, Wonder Woman

The hardest days for me are when I have this overwhelming desire to stay in my room and hide. My room has not only our bed, which is beautiful and even has linen sheets, but also my desk is in here where I work.

This is my safe place. It's my place where I can avoid facing the things that make me uncomfortable. That can be good or bad, depending.

I'm one of those people that wishes I could hide in here, away from everyone that challenges me, or everyone that needs something from me.

In here, I can put my earbuds in and listen to my Jesus music. But Ugh. People knock on the door. They text, they call, they message me on Messenger and Instagram and Snapchat.

I often want to throw the phone away. That is the real me. That's the "me" that lives in my head a lot of the time. I feel like some of you may relate to this. Don't think that I'm this super extrovert woman that easily talks to everyone and is always ready to engage. I'm not.

I have to push myself out of my comfort zone. I can't tell you how many times I've heard one of our girls coming down the hall, or in from the front door and I close my door because I just can't do it. Then, I hate myself for it and question if I'm even up to the ministry we began!

The fact is, I'm not up for it. It's God who carries me. I have these conversations with Him that would probably shock some folks. I'm very frank, even with Him. I say things like "You Know I am weak! I need you to show up today!" Followed by, "I know you always show up. I'm sorry!"

I tell him to please help my unbelief! Help me to trust more. Help me to get up and move.

And He does.

I often return to an Elisabeth Elliot quote "Just do the next thing" to keep me taking the next step.

I look ahead in my calendar and have that sense of dread come over me. I have a lot of appointments ahead. And I don't really even understand why I feel this way sometimes. I love people.

I love to meet people and I love to help people. I just think for me, it's there to help me remember that I'm totally dependent on God for all of it. I cannot do this. Sometimes, I feel as though I can't do the simplest task.

There are small baby steps you can begin to take. I'll list a few to get you started.

1. Write a note to someone that you know is struggling and drop it in the mail to them.

2. Ask a new mom if you can come clean her house for her, or even just the kitchen!

3. Take a meal, or just a gift card for a meal, to someone you know is either sick or hungry.

4. Pick some wildflowers and take them to an older woman who can't get out.

5. Keep some non-perishables or gift cards for fast food, in your car for the times when you see someone begging on the road.

6. Do something kind for someone you live with. One thing! Die to yourself for just one thing.

7. Send a text to someone that says you love them and are praying for them today. Then pray on the spot!

8. Have some gas gift cards available for when you see someone needs help with some gas.

9. Empty the dishwasher! This is my favorite. I hate to empty the dishwasher!

10. Ask someone what you can do to help them today.

Those are some suggestions that could get you started. It doesn't take much to show another person kindness.

We all must get out of our own worlds and look to see how we can help.

Kindness will change the world.

45
"Ma's Not Gonna Like That"

Would I rather be feared or loved? Easy. Both.
I want people to be afraid how much they love me.
- Michael Scott, The Office

When a new girl arrives at TWM, everyone is a little nervous. For me, the word "nervous" is a gross understatement. I'm petrified! It takes time for the new girl to assimilate into the family and the way we do things.

Some things, I take a slow and easy wins the race approach. But some other things, have to be dealt with head-on, right from the start. One example is racism. I will not tolerate it, even for a moment. One girl decided to use the "n" word a few times, but of course, not in my hearing. Only in front of the sisters.

I confronted her about it and told her that she is absolutely not to use that word here. Well, she did it again. For her consequences, I made her watch the movie Twelve Years A Slave. I'd hoped that watching that would make her at least begin to see the injustice inflicted on African Americans and have some heart to not use that word.

To my dismay, she was totally unmoved. She even fast forwarded through the singing of the Spirituals. She did stop using the word though because everyone would come down on her when she used it.

Since patience is not my strongest attribute, I developed for myself a few "rules" to live by. One of them was, if it can be dealt with later, then do it later because emotions have often calmed down, later.

Another one was, to remind myself to put myself in their place before I react. That would always add some time to my already short fuse. In almost any issue or problem that would arise around here, the whole family would eventually know about it.

There's no way to keep many secrets. So, one of the hard parts for me is when everyone gives their input to what I should think or do. Sometimes my head would spin at all the "suggestions."

I get it from Marcus and Alex too. Especially them! And they're the ones whose opinions I value the most! But when it comes in a barrage because emotions are high, I feel the weight of it so much that I want to crawl in a hole. You add in all the residents here and sometimes it feels like too much to bear.

One of the immediate, no-patience-at-all-given things is that we have anonymity here when it comes to guys.

I don't want some random dude you met to be told where we live. Do not let some stranger guy drive you home, because then he'll know where TWM is.

How more clearly can I put it? One girl got asked to move out partly because she walked some guy right up to our house! The safety of my family and the girls that live here are of the utmost importance. Don't do it. Their guy friend choices are sometimes drug dealers and users.

One time, I had taken a girl's phone away because I had an inkling she was communicating with her baby's daddy (and I use that word - daddy - loosely) who was abusive. Around midnight, I saw the phone light up. I got up, picked up the phone. Low and behold, not only did he text her, he was right in front of the house!

I have absolutely no patience for lying. Do not lie to me. Ma doesn't like that. I can take anything you have to say, but it better be the truth. You can't shock me. You can't make me run away from you or hate you. But it doggone better be honest.

If you're home after 10:00 pm, and I ask you where you've been, you're better off with the truth (no matter how bad) than a lie, because I will find out. Lying patterns will find you in a new place of residence, other than TWM. I have to have some level of trust, for you to live here with my disabled son.

Another thing I don't like is graphic nudity or sex on the TV. This pregnant girl lived here once and she was so excited that we had Netflix. She propped herself up on the sofa one day and turned on something she's been dying to watch.

Alex walked in and asked what she was watching. "Orange Is The New Black" she replied. Alex said "Ohhh, Ma's not gonna like that."

We aren't going to have porn or "soft porn" airing on the TV's of TWM. It's an absolute no. There are many reasons for this; some are obvious. I monitor what shows are watched in the house. There is no *Game Of Thrones* here. I'm not judgmental of you that watch it. I just don't want it here. I don't think it honors God to watch it.

Ma is OCD. It's a problem and one that having these lovely women move in here has largely cured me of. But I hold my ground on a few things. Wash your hands after using the potty and also before opening the refrigerator. I will remind the girls if I didn't see it or hear it.

Those situations can be very awkward. Especially when a hygiene-challenged girl lives here and yells when I remind her. I have thrown away whole blocks of cheese because they were handled with unwashed hands. Hygiene isn't going to be conquered overnight. There are ways I can curtail the awkward moments when someone is new.

I offer to make them something! That way, they don't handle the food for everybody. I ask them to handwash something for me! That'll secretly get their hands washed! We avoid humiliation while they're learning.

166

46
Ma and Pa: A United Front

A good marriage is where each partner secretly suspects
they got the better deal.
- Anonymous

Pa: Ma, you seem hyper from your caffeine this morning

Ma: Well, Pa, it sure beats your low-key 'ludes!

My first concert was the Christian singer Sandi Patty, and Marcus went to see Eric Clapton; that should tell you something right there.

It also says that as different as we are in musical tastes and other opinions, we are a united front in our home.

At night we prop up in bed and while he reads thick theology books, I watch murder on *Dateline*.

Opposites attract. Opposites fill in each other's gaps. When you have a team consisting of an extrovert and an introvert, it means everything gets said that needs to be said, and every important decision has the quiet moment of reflection it deserves.

Pa was once a pipefitter and then he was a Pastor. Now he's the full-time TWM Administrator, my Rock of Gibraltar, and my ballast on windy days.

47
Around the Table

*We live in a post-Christian world that is sick and tired of
hearing from Christians. But who could argue with
mercy-driven hospitality?*
- Rosaria Butterfield, *The Gospel Comes with a House Key*

Probably the number one way you can make a difference
in someone's life when they are hurting, depressed, lonely, poor, downtrodden, marginalized, or in need some
other way, is to have them in your home and around
your table, looking at one another face to face, over conversation, while eating a meal.

I don't know exactly why but it seems to be where faith
and love for one another grows. It's almost magical. It's
supernatural.

A beautiful table with delicious food that God has provided for our enjoyment as well as our nutrition, while in
each other's company, is just the best.

Jesus is present there.

The central place in this house is the huge table in the
kitchen. I talk about it often because that table has seen
so much. Some of the meals have been huge feasts and in
more lean times, a place of delicious beans and rice. It's
also been a place of hard conversations, lots of laughter
and many tears.

It's there that we sat with a girl estranged from her father, with him on the other side, trying to help build some bridges.

It's here where we come together after a hard week and love one another over Ma's lasagna.

It's there that we've laughed and cried together.

It's there where we've sat in silence because everyone is angry.

It's here where we've listened to many hurting people talk of their pain.

It's there where we pray and bless his name for the food.

On special occasions, we have sung the Doxology as "grace" before we begin eating.

Praise God from whom all blessings flow.
Praise Him all creatures, here below.
Praise Him above ye heavenly hosts.
Praise Father, Son and Holy Ghost.
Amen

Usually, it's Pa as the Chief Servant of the house, that has the privilege of thanking the Lord for the food.

The table has some holes beaten into it from a little two year old boy who lived here years ago

To my horror, he would bang his fork into the wood, repeatedly. His mother never seemed to notice.

Theo bangs his fists there when we play his favorite song, "The Sound Of Silence" By Disturbed. If you've never heard their version, try it. The volume must be up very high. His voice. Wow.

I have a video of two of our girls singing and dancing on one of the benches of the table just holding hands and dying laughing. I can't count the number of times we've played board games there, until late into the night, usually when my birthed kids are in town.

The table is where one of our girls decided to yell at Pa. She had enough of him holding her accountable. I don't even remember what it was about. Everyone that heard it (Ok, yes, we were at the bottom of the stairs listening) was jaw dropped! You don't yell at Pa! Well, I can, but I'm the only one.

This house is nothing to look at. It's comfortable and cozy but the attractive thing about it is the life that's here. Messed up, broken, loving people, gathering around a beat up old table in the kitchen. It's life. I'll take this life over a gorgeous, perfect house and table any day of the week. I was the one that used to cry when something got broken. Now, I just shrug it off. This old house is beat up. But everyone always corrects me and says it's beautiful, especially the table.

48
Conservative or Liberal

Extremes to the right and to the left are always wrong.
- Dwight D. Eisenhower

Scott Sauls once said, "I'm too liberal for my conservative friends and too conservative for my liberal friends."

I really feel the same way. Friends of mine don't appreciate this "liberal" turn I've made. I understand where they're coming from because I used to be there.

I don't think I've become liberal at all. I still believe that we're sinners, saved only by grace, and that someone truly saved by grace, will not stay in their sin, but be convicted of that sin by the Holy Spirit, turn from it (also by His power) and live a more godly life. BUT, where my views have changed is, now I see that not everyone has my experience in life.

There are people out there that have had horrific childhoods, some in poverty, some surrounded by drugs, hunger, no parental affection, etc. and these people, are coming from a totally different place than I am.

I had two loving parents. I had a very white, middle class, Christian upbringing where my only problem was having to clean the bathroom each Saturday instead of getting to watch my cartoons!

So, it would be easy for me to say (as I used to!) "Y'all just do the right thing for once!" Or "Why in the world would you live that way?" "You can't possibly know God!"

That is a very proud person speaking. That's someone that looks down on the problems of others. That is not Jesus-like. I began to see how hard and cold my heart was and I decided that I don't want to be that person anymore.

Thoughts still come into my mind from the old me and I push them away as fast as I can. Those thoughts make me sick to my stomach. So, when people hear me cheering on the girl that is promiscuous or the girl that's an addict, I'm not saying "Stay like you are!" I'm saying "Come with me! We both need his mercy!"

These girls will often look at me and laugh. They'd say "What have you ever done wrong?" I love to answer that question because while I didn't use drugs and I have been with the same man for 36 years, I tell them about Proverbs 6:16-19.

"There are six things the Lord hates, seven that are detestable to him: Proud looking eyes, a lying tongue, hands that shed innocent blood, a heart that devises wicked schemes, feet that are quick to rush into evil, a false witness who pours out lies, and a person who stirs up conflict in the community."

Then I ask them what is the very first thing that the Lord hates. Is it murder? Is it lying? Is it wicked schemes? No. It's pride. My favorite of all sins. So, I need mercy too, just as much, if not more than they do.

Once they see the love and mercy of Jesus, their hearts open up to him and he changes them from the inside out. Sometimes this is a fast change and sometimes it's much slower. That's where patience comes in.

Patience has long been my enemy. My family can attest to this. But God! He has tested my patience time and time again, forcing me to grow. I only grow through tough things. I only grow through him dragging me, kicking and screaming.

I have a friend of many years whose life growing up was truly something I could have never imagined. She endured a horrific childhood. Her mother was, for a time, involved in witchcraft. She was pimped out by a close relative at 14. Episodes of rape also plagued her early adult life. Cocaine numbed her pain. She worked as a night club dancer. Her first abortion came around this time.

Some people like to act as if an abortion doesn't traumatize a woman. Every woman I've known that has had an abortion has been severely traumatized by it. The regret and the fantasizing about the "what if's" is like a plague that comes and goes in waves. "What would that child look like today?"

Or, they dread the anniversary of the day they did it. They remember their baby's due date and see it as the birthday lost! Sure, some can stuff it down and move on to some degree, but not entirely.

My friend came to Christ through her sister a few years later. She was so passionate about her new-found Savior! She learned and grew and moved forward in her journey.

Old sins and habits don't just disappear automatically. Maturing takes time and hard circumstances.

She became pregnant again. Now what? Does she have a baby out of wedlock in an unforgiving Christian community? How would they see her? How do you carry the shame in church with a growing belly and no ring on your left hand? What did she do? She had another abortion.

And while that makes me sad for her and her unborn baby, it also is a rallying call to action. What if the church had been a place of refuge for her? What if she knew in her heart that she would not be shamed, but loved and cared for.

That, my friends, is not an approval for sexual relations outside of marriage. Instead, it is loving someone toward Jesus. Isn't that what we want? Do you know anyone that was berated and shamed into loving Jesus? I sure don't.

I hear pro-life people say things like "A Christian would never abort their baby" or on social media they declare that "Abortion is murder!" I get their passion for the unborn and I also have passion for the unborn, but the way it's done absolutely does more damage to the dear souls of the women that have experienced it and likely doesn't actually do any good for the unborn.

Wouldn't it be better to actually help pregnant women, so they have options? Many abortions take place because women don't see any options. Wouldn't it be better to give love and support to a woman traumatized by abortion? If people want to end abortion, then I say do something to help. Please, if you're not already actively working in some way to help these women, then please get involved. You are so needed!

I also believe that part of being pro-life is not only caring for the unborn, but also the already born. It means caring for the prisoner, the condemned, the poor, the sick, the orphan and widow! The most vulnerable among us.

I believe that the Evangelical Conservative Right has gotten more political than Jesus-like. I want no part of it. I'm not saying Christians shouldn't be in politics. I'm saying that the religious, evangelical, conservative movement is a religion of it's own and it needs to be abandoned. It's an idol of our day, and it stinks with corruption, wickedness, power hungry, money driven people that I will not align with. That's not to say that I won't vote for a Republican at times but I also might vote for a Democrat at times.

People say that you can't be pro-life and vote for a Democrat. I used to say it! I told someone, many years ago, that because they voted for a Democratic presidential candidate, that they had baby's blood on their hands. It makes me shudder to think about saying that to someone. I'm so sorry!

Now, I see a more broad and clearer picture. Being pro-life is more than abortion. It's also caring for the African American men and women in the prison system that got a bad deal because they were black and poor. Or maybe working to care for the orphaned children everywhere.

It's also about caring for the hungry! Let's build residences for the homeless instead of multi-million dollar fancy church buildings. We don't need churches with marble and crystal. Being pro-life means being there for the living everywhere!

Here I stand. I'm too conservative for my liberal friends and too liberal for my conservative friends. I don't fit in anywhere.

I don't believe Jesus did either.

49
A Mother's Heartache

Maybe 'letting go with love', means letting go of the silence.
- Sandy Swenson

Any mother of a drug addict will understand.

I have a daughter that inflicts pain, upon pain, upon pain. Do other mothers get the release of hatred that comes vomiting out of her mouth again and again? Are all addicts this vicious? I don't know. I only know my own experience.

This happened yesterday.

My phone began ringing and as is my practice, I don't answer calls from people that aren't in my contact information. This one also wasn't, but it was from a 208 area code so I knew it had to either be her or be about her. My throat got constricted and my heart began beating rapidly.

I let it ring several times, debating whether I wanted to answer it.

"Hello?"

"Hello Mrs. Rench, this is Jill. I'm a friend of Kat's. She's in jail."

Jill went on to tell me that Kat's bond was one thousand dollars and a bail bondsman was one hundred fifty dollars after fees. She was asking me to bail Kat out.

Can you imagine what this is like for a mother? My daughter was in jail and unless someone bailed her out, she would spend over a month there, awaiting her court date. I'm not gonna lie, I was tempted to do it. But I also know that if I bailed her out, she would be able to use meth again. Inside jail, she'd have a harder time getting it, at least.

I also knew that if I didn't do it, she would spew more toxic venom at me and anyone else that would listen to her lie about me. Nobody wants that. So, I told Jill that I'd consider it but that I needed to talk to her dad first.

Jill called me back the next morning. She said Kat had hung up on her for not getting her out sooner. She also had a few choice words for me.

She began talking about how she had been a strung-out meth addict but that God had saved her because people were praying for her. Sounded great to me!

"Wonderful!" I'd said.

She asked if I knew Jesus. I assured her that I did, and I began getting an ominous feeling. Clearly Kat had been telling her for a while, what a worthless mother I am.

You should know that Kat is a brilliant manipulator. She's manipulated me like a pro for so long.

She continued, "I know you have a ministry to women and it's clear that you're distracted from your own daughter by your work with these women." It was a low blow. I was speechless, momentarily. Then, I decided to fight back because that is not true and I'm tired of being Kat's punching bag.

"Wait a minute! Hold on here! I am not distracted from my daughter and her addiction. I'm just not going to be scammed into enabling her any more." I endured twenty minutes of torturous lecturing about my first born child and how I should love her (as if I don't). The patronizing, passive aggressive stabs that rendered me broken again.

It's like that scene from *Indiana Jones*, where the voodoo leader would literally rip out a person's heart, straight from his chest with his bare hands. But in this case, it's then thrown down to the ground and stomped on.

I'm just tired, y'all. It's been so many years of this. How do I tuck in back in where I can not feel again?

What's a mother to do? Give in to her daughter's whims and help her use so she will like me? Use tough love that doesn't buy meth for her, because I love her that much?

If you're a mother of an addict, you will understand the emotional rollercoaster.

179

50
Selective Gratitude: Donations We Would've Been Happy Not Receiving.

One man's trash is another man's treasure

People have been very good to us, and I mean, very good. Folks have donated money, critically-needed items and best of all, groceries.

I am so thankful for it. I want to highlight those things but I thought I'd take a minute and mention some "other" things that have been donated to TWM. I'm not trying to be ungrateful, but maybe a little instructive to donors of nonprofits everywhere!

This is a list of the more interesting things that we've received, for your edification and for your entertainment!

1. Used (and very worn, even stained) underwear and bras.

2. A bed with three legs.

3. A very used car seat with feces on it.

4. Yard toys that had been in a yard for a decade or more.

5. Ripped up sofas

6. Old, filthy furniture

7. Boxes of broken dishes that had been in a garage and sprayed by a cat for years.

8. Tons and tons of garbage bags full of old, stained ruined clothes.

9. Outdated deli baked goods

10. Outdated canned yams

11. Very old towels and linens

12. Strawberries with mold on them.

13. 25 expired Food Lion deli pies

14. Half empty bottles of shampoo

15. A large bag of used shoes that some didn't even have a match to.

16. Freezer-burned frozen meat.

I could go on and on. I cannot tell you how many trips to the dump Marcus and Theo have made. It's just one more unnecessary thing to have to do. Now, I know everyone thinks their stuff is great. But you gotta realize that I want my girls to know that they are worth more than used, old, stained, dingy thongs to wear. And I'm not going to feed them stale Food Lion donuts. I'm just not.

If you want to give someone a car seat, please for the love of everything holy, wash the cover first. Throw away the expired yams and other canned goods. My girls will eat fresh foods. And as of this date, none of them have had only one foot, so the shoes need a match if they're to be helpful.

It makes me wonder if some people think so low of these women that they think they should be grateful for anything. Actually, they probably would be, but I'm not for them. They're worth so much more than that.

I don't mean to be harsh, I really don't. But think about it. You want to buy a new item to replace your old, worn out one, so give it to The Welcome Mission! They'll take anything! What if you kept the worn out one and donated the new one to these women?

Imagine that?

51
Not My First Rodeo: The TWM Application

TWM is not a free hotel for you to do whatever you want.
- Ma

Imagine having one or two people (an adult and their child) move in with your family with very little notice, like right as you are settling down for the night: lights out, stove off, doors locked.

Oh, who can that be ringing the doorbell?

Welcome to our world.

Here are the questions on our application:

Name:

Date Of Birth:

What Social Media sites are you on, including dating sites?

Have you ever been convicted of a felony? If so, what is the charge?

Do you have ANY pending charges now? If so, what are they?

Do you have children in your custody? If so, what age(s)?

Do you have any mental health diagnoses? YES/NO

Do you have any medical diagnoses? YES/NO

Do you take medication? YES/NO If YES, please list:

What is your current living situation?

Do you have a driver's license?

Do you have transportation?

These questions have evolved over the years from a lot of experience. These are, in my estimation, the most important things I need to know about a girl.

For example, if a girl takes daily medication, that medication will have to go either into the safe, which is in my room, or in a locked box they own. There is no wiggle room here, unless it's something temporary like antibiotics. Girls who have worked hard over the years, finding ways to get high will steal anything and everything if it's left out in front of them.

If the medicine is of a certain variety, for example, if it's used to treat the more serious mental illnesses, then I will not likely invite her to live here. I can't manage someone's meds because I'm not qualified medical personnel.

184

The dating sites are also of concern for me. Plenty of Fish, Tinder and Whisper are the ones that girls in our past have utilized for casual hookups. This puts them in danger as well as the whole family when the location of TWM is given out.

Dating and dating sites are absolutely not allowed at TWM. I have a few "profiles" of my own under false names so I can stalk and make sure my girls aren't on them. This is not my first rodeo.

When some girls come to me, I just know they're going to be here. I can tell. But still I pray about it. Sometimes I've prayed silently while I'm sitting across from them, or I might take a few days, and approach my board as well for input.

Also, some I've brought in sight unseen because they're daughters or granddaughters of old friends. My heart goes out even more when they're people I've known for a long time. There's more connection.

So, the process is, if a girl comes to the point of interest in coming here to live, I send them this "application" of sorts for them to fill out. Once they do come, they will also sign a document saying that they're aware that there are surveillance cameras in and around the house and that they agree with that. Lastly, they will sign a document saying that they will abide by the rules of the house and that if they don't, it could result in Ma uninviting them to live here.

52
What We've Done Well

For when I hear the praises start
I want to rain upon you
Blessings that will fill your heart
I see no stain upon you
Because you are my child and you know me
To Me you're only holy
Nothing that you've done remains
Only what you do for Me.
- Keith Green, "When I Hear the Praises Start"

Writing a book has allowed me to consider our work here at TWM in a holistic way. There are many things we've done well, things I'm very proud of. Things that I don't normally even remember on a day to day basis.

Like the time that I was able to convince a girl, that had been estranged from her parents for years, to go see her dad now that he was dying. I took her. We went that day. She saw him, wept with him, hugged him, made peace with him. He died days later. I'm proud of that. That was one of the best days I've had working with TWM.

Or the time I called Child Protective Services on a mom to have her son taken away because he was in danger. As I talked to the lady on the phone, I was crying so hard she couldn't understand my words. I had to calm down to explain. That was so very hard to do. But it was the right thing to do and I'm proud of that.

There is at least one baby that's alive because of what we've accomplished here. There are many children whose lives are more promising and their futures are lovely and likely will be for generations to come.

Several people have come to Christ through this weak bumbling servant of the Lord.

God had to bring me low to make me look up. I wasn't someone he could use for his glory. I was proud, arrogant and self-righteous. I had to have some hard things happen to me for me to be usable.

Our first born daughter and her problems have been by far, the hardest trials in my life. For so many years now, it's been a struggle to just breathe at times.

You learn to lean-in to Jesus or risk dying. When you have a child that hates you and is destroying herself with drugs and any manner of other self destructive behaviors, you learn to survive.

My daughter has become someone I don't even know and she doesn't know me. This was my baby that I carried in my womb and nurtured, even fed from my own breast. And she is a stranger. This beautiful young woman, has been destroyed by this lifestyle that she will not walk away from.

If you can't tell already, my work here is very personal. If I can make a difference for one person, it's worth it.

187

It's my heart. It's my passion. Giving a girl with a sex addiction a place to live and find acceptance -- not for her destructive choices of the past -- but acceptance for her, is what I will do. Helping Vanessa get to where she is now, is something I'm damn proud of.

Helping a homeless, meth addict get clean and back to her kids is life changing for the three kids and their mom! I'm proud of that.

Helping save a child from an abusive mom and one that would have taken him from man to man and helping him get adopted by a great family. That makes me feel good for him and his future. He now has a chance.

We helped a pregnant mom and her boyfriend get married and off welfare. They had previously never had one marriage in their family that they could remember. Everyone just hooked up, made babies and went on.

Marriage wasn't even on their radar. But they accepted Jesus, got married, both work to the point where they don't even receive food stamps any more!

They're still married years later and even had another baby. I am so very proud of that. We were a small part of their lives changing.

We were instruments of Jesus in their lives and they're family will be affected for generations because of it. That's a reason to cheer!

We've been a part of countless smaller things as well. Even just the act of giving a heroin addict some food because she was wasting away due to lack of nutrition. I remember it like it was yesterday because she was so emaciated and sad.

We were standing in the laundry room where the food pantry is, downstairs. I put my hands on each side of her face and asked her what drugs she was using. At first she denied it but tears welled up in her eyes and in mine as we both knew that we knew. I gave her food and when she thanked me, I told her that it was from Jesus. She said, "You're amazing." And I said, 'No, He is amazing."

Did I do anything to change her life on a huge level? No. But I did get to show her the love and mercy of God. All it took was twenty minutes of my time, love in my heart, and some Mac and Cheese.

Or the time I took a teenage girl to Walgreens to buy a pregnancy test because she thought she was pregnant and couldn't tell her mother. She wasn't by the way, but she needed someone to help her without judgment and that's what we did. Let's not ever again say that a pregnancy out of wedlock is a consequence of bad behavior.

A baby is never a bad consequence. A baby is always a blessing. And frankly, I'm weary of the stigma on women who've had to carry the shame since the beginning of time, for an unplanned pregnancy, as if she impregnated herself, by herself. That would be hard to do!

TWM has done quite a lot of good over the years. We've accomplished good things because of the work of the Holy Spirit in our lives. I'm thankful for it and I hope we can continue. Here's to the next twenty-five!

Postscript

I'm Still Dreaming

My vision for the future is two-fold.

First, we want to expand! We recently walked through a huge antebellum house beside Johnson Pond on thirteen acres, and dreamed of TWM owning it. In a house that size, we counted room for us and twelve women. And the coolest part was that for years, it had been used as a home for women in need, in the late 1800's. I wanted it so badly!

I kept picturing in my mind's eye, a woman that has never felt she deserved anything good in her life, driving up that drive-way with her eyes huge at this beautiful house God provided for her to live in! I'm not into anything fancy, but I do want my girls to feel special, loved and valued.

I want for them to know that we love them, but more importantly, that Jesus loves them and fights for them. I wanted them to have access to animals on the property to care for, like horses for their anxiety, and a garden to tend outdoors! I'm still a dreamer. Can't you picture it too?

So, we hired a fund-raiser with hopes to see what would happen. Not one dime was raised.

Alright, so we must wait on the Lord for His timing and His plan. I just feel like my plan is so much better! Just kidding.

Secondly, Marcus and I want to speak to churches. We want to inspire and then teach people how to have Welcome Missions all over the country. We want to use what we've learned, often the hard way, to help others replicate it.

We want to inspire people to give sacrificially to make a difference in people's lives. Not everyone can have a Welcome Mission in their home, I get that. But everyone can be open and willing to God's call on their lives to love their neighbor in a more sacrificial way.

Will you join in prayer with us for the women we serve, the future of TWM and the finances needed to expand in some way? Will you be willing to be monthly donors, partnering with us?

We have people donating anywhere from ten dollars a month, up to over one thousand a month. Any amount is appreciated. Our budget is always tight and we also need large sums to buy a larger building or two!

I continue to dream.

For Jesus Christ, and for all the lost and lonely women out there. To Him be the glory.

Appendix

Acknowledgements
Holly's Reading Table
TWM Recipes
TWM Playlist
About the Author

Acknowledgements

There are many people that held me up through these years including TWM board members that have served behind the scenes. These folks have all been such an encouragement and help to me. I also want to thank our donors. We have never gone without what we need because of you.

My two friends and board members that have been with me for over 20 years, Laura Jacimore and Lourianne Hunt. They've always been there for me when I need help and they're faithful prayer partners for not only me, but for our girls.

I want to specifically thank two other dear women that have had my back. Kelly Hagood and Pamela Drane. For the many countless hours of back porch talking, lunches, coffee at The Mill etc. I always knew I could text you and you'd be there for me.

I would have never accomplished this without my editor and coach Jon Obermeyer. He has taken all my notes that I've gathered throughout the years and turned them into a book. He also has put up with my roller coaster personality quite well. He's a good encourager and newfound friend. He also didn't fuss too much when I turned the entire manuscript pink and didn't know how to fix it!

Lastly, to my husband, Marcus. Thank you for putting up with me. After 36 years, you're still the one I reach for.

Holly's Reading Table: Helpful & Related Books

I read *A Chance To Die* on the beach one year while on a vacation. I couldn't put it down. I read it through many tears. It is to date, besides the Bible, the most influential book on my life. Amy Carmichael was someone I greatly admire and aspire to be like.

Allender, Dan, *Bold Love*, 1992, NavPress.

Bonhoeffer, Dietrich, *Life Together: The Classic Exploration of Christian in Community*, 2009, HarperOne.

Butterfield, Rosaria, *The Gospel Comes with a House Key: Practicing Radically Ordinary Hospitality in Our Post-Christian World*, 2018, Crossway.

Carmichael, Amy, *If*, 1992, CLC Ministries.

Deere, Jack, *Even in Our Darkness: A Story of Beauty in a Broken Life*, 2018, Zondervan.

Desmond, Matthew, *Evicted: Poverty and Profit in the American City*, 2017, Broadway Books.

Elliot, Elisabeth, *A Chance to Die: The Life and Legacy of Amy Carmichael*, 1987, Revell.

Keller, Timothy, *The Prodigal Prophet: Jonah and the Mystery of God's Mercy*, 2018, Viking.

Langberg, Diane Mandt, *Counseling Survivors of Sexual Abuse, 1997,* (AACC Library), Tyndale House Publishers.

Lobert, Annie, *Fallen,* 2016, Worthy Press.

Mall, E. Jane, *Kitty, My Rib: The Heartwarming Story of a Woman of Courage and Devotion,* 1959, Concordia Publishing. My favorite book as a teenager!

Peck, M. Scott, *People of the Lie: The Hope for Healing Human Evil,* M. Scott Peck. 1998, Touchstone.

Ray, Charles, *Mrs. C.H. Spurgeon,* 2000, Christian Book Gallery.

Reinhart, Paula, *Sex and the Soul of a Woman,* 2004, 2010, Zondervan.

Sauls, Scott, *Jesus Outside the Lines: A Way Forward for Those Who Are Tired of Taking Sides,* 2015, Tyndale House Publishers, Inc.

Stevens, Todd, Stevens, Erin, *How to Pick Up a Stripper and Other Acts of Kindness: Serving People Just as They Are,* 2014, Refraction.

Stevenson, Bryan, *Just Mercy: A Story of Justice and Redemption,* 2014, Spiegel & Grau.

Tisby, Jemar, *The Color of Compromise: The Truth about the American Church's Complicity in Racism,* 2019, Zondervan.

Tripp, Paul David, *Instruments in the Redeemer's Hands: People in Need of Change Helping People in Need of Change*, 2002, P&R Publishing.

Vanier, Jean, *The Broken Body: Journey to Wholeness*, 1999, Darton Longman & Todd Ltd.

Voskamp, Anne, *One Thousand Gifts: A Dare to Live Fully Right Where You Are*, 2014, Zondervan.

Welch, Ed, *Side by Side: Walking with Others in Wisdom and Love*, 2015, Crossway.

All the Kay Scarpetta books by Patricia Cornwell.

Recipes from TWM

Creating a home-like atmosphere involves attention to meal planning and the meals themselves. For your benefit, I'm including nine recipes for some of the hands-down favorite meals that we serve.

Ma's Lasagna

I make lasagna pretty regularly. I don't follow a recipe specifically. So, this is the basic sauce. You can play around with it and make it your own. If you use the right ingredients, you almost can't go wrong. Imported canned tomatoes are a must. They're just better. You can use the brand I use or another, but these are my favorite. Also, I buy good pasta that is not necessary to pre-cook.

For the sauce:
4 lbs. Ground beef
1 lb. Ground sausage
2 28 oz. cans Cento San Marzano canned tomatoes (diced).
2 14 oz. cans Cento San Marzano canned tomato sauce.
2 tbsp. imported tomato paste
Lots of fresh basil, pulled off the stems (don't chop them).
Fresh garlic (sometimes I use powdered).

The cheeses:
6 to 8 cups whole milk mozzarella
2 cups good, grated parmesan
1 large whole milk ricotta

Cooking
Brown all the meat together and drain excess fat. Throw in everything else. Salt generously. It takes a few tablespoons. Sometimes I add in a half bottle of good red wine, if I didn't drink it all the night before.

Simmer sauce for several hours, covered.

Mix the cheeses up in large bowl.

Once the sauce is cooled down some, you're ready to build!

Grease a large lasagna pan. Spray the inside with Pam and begin layering the sauce, pasta and cheese mixture, ending with sauce. Add a coat of good parmesan on top and bake at 375 for about an hour, uncovered.

Garlic Stuffed Pork Loin With Apricot Glaze

Whole Pork Loin (never use a half because it will have
the dark meat cut off and the meat will be dry).
1 bottle Soy Sauce
2 whole pods fresh garlic, minced
3 tablespoons red pepper
2 tablespoons coarse kosher salt
2 tablespoons water
1 medium jar Apricot Preserves

Marinate the whole loin in the soy sauce overnight. In the
morning, pour off remaining sauce. Place the loin in large
baking dish. Cut (lengthways) two-inch slivers into the
meat all over (making sure every piece will have some).

Mix garlic, salt, red pepper and water into a paste.

With your fingers, stuff the slits with the paste mixture.

With any remaining paste, rub it all over the meat.

Cover tightly and bake at 300 degrees for 5 hours. Then,
take out of oven and put one half of the jar of preserves
all over the meat. Cover and cook for 30 more minutes.
Take out of oven and place on a platter covered with a
bed of cooked rice. Pour the liquid around the meat all
over it and the rice. Spoon the rest of the preserves all
over the meat.

Garnish with sprigs of fresh Rosemary.

Spicy Dried Lentil Dip

From the Kitchen: Crock Pot

Ingredients and Preparation

These can be varied dramatically! I often throw in all sorts of different things, depending on what I have available that would go with the flavors.

Add 1.5 large boxes of chicken broth to 1 pound lentils.

Add chopped onions, peppers and lots of garlic.

Add 1 can chipotle peppers in adobo sauce. I use La Costena brand.

Add Mexican spices (you can use a few packets of taco seasoning if you want to).

Add a ham steak chopped into small bites.

Simmer for a few hours until tender.

Let them cool. The mixture should thicken up.

Put the mixture into pie plates and top with shredded cheese. Use for dipping. They can also be covered and frozen for future use.

Sunday Salad

Pa is a master smoker of meat. He built his own smoker, so on Sundays, we often have a smoked pork butt or something like that.

I began making my "Sunday Salads" about 20 years ago. The key is first, presentation. So, it must go on a huge platter. -- never a bowl.

3 Heads Romaine Lettuce, washed, dried and chopped.
Red, Yellow and Orange peppers, sliced thin; sweet onion very thinly sliced.
Cherry tomatoes
2 packages Feta Cheese, crumbled
Bacon bits (generous amount)
Crispy onion salad toppers or crispy jalapenos
Cardini's Caesar Dressing in abundance

Creamy Chicken Breasts

Ingredients
4 boneless, skinless Chicken Breasts
8 slices Swiss Cheese
1 can Cream of Chicken Soup
¼ cup White Wine
2 cups crushed Pepperidge Farm Herb Seasoned Stuffing
¼ cup Butter

Preparation
Lay breasts in greased pyrex. Mix soup and wine together and pour over salted and peppered breasts. Add the swiss cheese slices to the top. Sprinkle stuffing over and melted butter.

Bake 350 for 40 to 45 minutes.

Crustless Keto Quiche

Ingredients
1 Package Canadian Bacon
5 Eggs
1 cup Cream
1 cup shredded Gouda cheese
1 bunch Asparagus (or whatever vegetables you want)
1 Onion, chopped
1 tsp. salt

Preparation
Grease a large pie pan. Line with Canadian Bacon. Beat eggs and add other ingredients. Pour into pie plate and bake 350 for about 40 to 45 minutes.

Chicken Enchiladas

This recipe has been made with so many variations!
You can use flour tortillas or corn. You can use canned
chicken or fresh. You can boil a whole chicken or just
white meat, or roast them. Either way, you'll debone the
meat and cut up in chunks. I prefer a roasted or crock pot
cooked whole chicken for this recipe. I recommend mix-
ing in the the dark meat with the white meat.

I like it spicy. You can make it more spicy, or less spicy.

Ingredients
1 Whole Chicken, roasted, cooled and chopped
2 onions, chopped
2 cans green chilis
3 tbsp. Butter
1 container Sour Cream
2 cups Jack Cheese, shredded
1 jar jalapenos
1 pint heavy cream

Preparation
Sautee onions and chilis in the butter. Add the sour cream
and chicken. Also add the jalapenos to your specification.
Spoon mixture into a tortilla and add some cheese.

Lay in buttered 9/13 casserole, side by side. Add remaining cheese on top. Before baking, pour 1 pint of cream
over top. Garnish with jalapenos and cilantro. Bake at 350
until bubbly

Crock Pot Sunday Roast

This is similar to the recipe passed down by my mom to me. I've changed it some over the years. It's the very first meal I made in 1983 when I first got married at 18 years old!

Ingredients
Large Chuck Roast
2 Cans Cream of Onion Soup
2 Packets Lipton Onion Soup Mix
Onions
Potatoes cut in big chunks

Preparation
Place the roast in the crock pot. Add potatoes and onions and then the rest of the ingredients.

Cook on high for 8 to 10 hours.

You can add whatever you like to this recipe.

The Best and Easiest Chicken Spaghetti Ever

Ingredients
1 Whole chicken
1 large Velveeta
2 cans Rotel tomatoes
1 ½ pound spaghetti pasta
Jalapenos if desired

Preparation
Boil a whole chicken until the meat will easily come off the bone. Cool and debone but save the water that the chicken was boiled in. It should not be a whole lot of water at this point.

Add the spaghetti to the chicken broth and cook most of the way. (You can scrape the layer of fat off the top first if you prefer) You will NOT dump out the remaining water after cooking the spaghetti. Instead, you'll add the chicken, 2 cans Rotel tomatoes and Velveeta Cheese, cut in chunks. Stir and let the cheese melt through.

Pour into greased casserole and bake uncovered. It will seem watery but after it comes out of the oven and cools some, the spaghetti will soak up the remaining liquid.

Add salt to taste

TWM Playlist

O come, let us sing unto the Lord: - Psalm 95:1

Music is a huge part of life here at TWM. We listen to music while we do dishes, while we're getting ready for church, out back on the porch on a cool fall evening, with the twinkly lights hanging above! Ma prefers her praise music, but sometimes she might force the girls to listen to her "Mellow Gold 70's Hits" playlist on Amazon.

1. When I Hear The Praises Start - Keith Green
2. Feast In The House Of Zion - Sandra McCracken
3. The Sound Of Silence - Disturbed
4. Boldly I Approach - Rend Collective
5. Voice Of Truth - Casting Crowns (My life song)
6. Fear Is A Liar - Zach Williams
7. Let It Rain - Michael W. Smith
8. Hold Me Jesus - Rich Mullins
9. Africa - Toto
10. Wood And Nails - The Porter's Gate
11. Georgia On My Mind - Ray Charles
12. Living Hope - Phil Wickham
13. Dancing In The Minefields - Andrew Peterson
14. You Are Good - Israel Houghton
15. He Is Alive - Third Day
16. Worn - Tenth Avenue North
17. How Great Thou art - Ascend The Hill
18. Holy Holy Holy- Sufjan Stevens
19. Jesus, Thank You - Sovereign Grace Music
20. At Last - Etta James

About the Author

Holly Rench is the Executive Director and co-founder of The Welcome Mission. She's been married to Marcus for 36 years. She's the mother of six children she and Marcus have had together, as well as countless other young adults she has "adopted" into their family.

She loves to cook and feed large groups of people in her home, which is a good thing considering the sentence above. Holly is passionate about her "kids" and all of her grandkids. Her feet hit the floor every morning with a burning drive to make a difference in the world for the marginalized, oppressed and the poor. That is her life's work.

This is her first book.

You can connect with Holly through The Welcome Mission web page TheWelcomeMission.org and also through Facebook at facebook.com/TheWelcomeMission/ to learn more about how you can get involved.

76740077R00126

Made in the USA
Columbia, SC
26 September 2019